DALE INGRAHAM
TEAR DOWN THIS WALL

SEXUAL ABUSE WITHIN THE CHURCH

outskirtspress
DENVER, COLORADO

The opinions expressed in this manuscript are solely the opinions of the author and do not represent the opinions or thoughts of the publisher. The author has represented and warranted full ownership and/or legal right to publish all the materials in this book.

Tear Down This Wall
Sexual Abuse Within The Church
All Rights Reserved.
Copyright © 2012 Dale Ingraham
v3.0 r1.0

Cover Design by Nathan Ingraham © 2012
Author Photo by Jeanette Ingraham © 2012. All rights reserved - used with permission.

This book may not be reproduced, transmitted, or stored in whole or in part by any means, including graphic, electronic, or mechanical without the express written consent of the publisher except in the case of brief quotations embodied in critical articles and reviews.

Outskirts Press, Inc.
http://www.outskirtspress.com

ISBN: 978-1-4327-9592-4

Library of Congress Control Number: 2012913448

Outskirts Press and the "OP" logo are trademarks belonging to Outskirts Press, Inc.

PRINTED IN THE UNITED STATES OF AMERICA

This book is dedicated to my wife, Faith, and all those who know the pain of abuse. I still remember the night at college not long before we were engaged when Faith told me that she had been raped and molested by her father. It was heart wrenching for her and I could tell that part of her was thinking that it would be easier to walk away from our relationship than to have to tell me what had happened. I can only imagine how many other girls out there have had to live through the same nightmare of not knowing what to say or how to say it. I often wonder, how many husbands and wives have never told their mates that they were abused because they were too afraid or embarrassed to tell.

Faith has been a great wife and mom. She has been at my side for my twenty nine years of ministry and has been a true 'help mate' for me. We founded 'Speaking Truth in love Ministries' in 2008 to address the issue of abuse in the Christian community and I enjoy partnering with her as we speak in churches, Bible Colleges and wherever God gives us an open door.

Table of Contents

Preface i

Introduction v

1. The Sin 1

2. The Victims 11
    Victim Stage 14
    Survivor Stage 18
    Victor Stage 21

3. The Offender 25
    Repentance and the Offender 25
    Confession and the Offender 30
    Religion and the Offender 31

4. The Enablers 37
    Direct Enablers 38
    Indirect Enablers 41

5. The Consequences 43

6. The Wall 50
    Fears that Build the Wall 52
    Steps to Tearing Down the Wall 67

7. The Church's Role in Dealing with Abuse 78

8. The Families' Role in Dealing with Abuse 97

9. The Victims' Role in Dealing with Abuse 108
    They Must Understand God's Love for Them................108
    They need to see themselves as God sees them............112
    They Must See God For Who He Is....................................116
    They Must Understand Their Identity in Christ 121

10. The Offender's Role in Dealing with Abuse 130
    Must find a place of repentance...132
    Must Make a True Confession..135
    Must Accept the Consequences of Their Sin 138
    Must Labor to Make Restitution 142
    Must Realize that Restoration does not mean
        that Everything goes back to the Way it was 144

11. The Truth 148
    The Truth About Forgiveness 148
    The Truth about Mercy...159
    The Truth About Grace 162
    The Truth About Love 167
    The Truth About Sin 171
    The Truth About Consequences...174

Preface

Many years ago as a prosecutor, God opened my eyes to the horrific realities of child sexual abuse. As I prepared cases for prosecution, I encountered so many precious souls that had given up all hope as a result of being victimized as a child. What I found even more disturbing was the reality that this dark and destructive crime has no boundaries, and is epidemic in size within the Christian community.

Why has the church been so silent about a sin that is destroying its community one soul at a time? In fact, far too often when child sexual abuse is discussed within the Protestant community, it is in the context of pointing the finger at our Catholic brothers and sisters. Pointing the finger at others is sadly the manner in which Protestants have been able to avoid addressing this darkness within its very own soul. Clinical psychologist, Mary Gail Frawley-O'Dea says, "The more profound the betrayal and the more vital to survival the betrayer is, the more likely it is that the trauma will be denied, dissociated, or diminished by both the victim and the bystander who consciously or unconsciously insist on maintaining an attachment to the victimizer on whom they depend for some aspect of survival, including at times spiritual survival." This quote has immensely helped me understand the failure of the Christian community to confront and address a sin that is prevalent and destructive. Christians too often deny, dissociate, or diminish this crime because we have elevated the perpetrators and the institution to a position that can only be filled by the righteous and holy God. When survivors come forward, the institution often feels threatened and immediately moves to protect the "Godly" perpetrator, while at the same time devalues and demonizes the very souls that need to be loved and embraced. I believe this monumental failure on the part of the Christian community is a consequence of its failure to understand and embrace the Gospel. The Gospel tells us that it is Christ's perfection, Christ's obedience, Christ's holiness, Christ's selflessness, (the list could go on and on and on) which reconciles dark and depraved sinners such as you and me with such a perfect, sovereign, and loving God. Put another way, it is the "good works" of Jesus, not us, that draws us into the arms of our Heavenly Father. The consequence of fully grasping and embracing this indescribable truth is that our identity is not in ourselves and what we do, but in Christ and what He has done. Therefore, when we seek to control and protect the institution we fail to understand the very fundamentals of the Gospel. This control and protectionism is often carried out under the guise of "protecting the integrity of the Gospel" when it reality it is nothing more than protecting the identity and reputation of the institution. Perhaps the most common method of such protectionism is secrecy and silence. An institutional centered church will do all it can to silence sin and those who expose it in order to protect its "reputation within the community". A Gospel centered church will embrace light and be transparent about sin. It will also lovingly embrace those wounded by sin, regardless of what others may think or say, understanding that its identity and reputation is in Christ alone.

Only a few times in one's life do we encounter saints who give up status, reputation, and even wealth in order to bring light to a dark area of the Christian world. Martin Luther, William Wilberforce and Dietrich Bonheoffer are just a few that come to mind. Another such saint that comes to mind is Dale Ingraham. I was so blessed to have the opportunity of meeting Dale and Faith Ingraham a couple of years ago at a conference. I was immediately struck by the burden God has placed upon their hearts to carry a bright light to a very dark and quiet place within the Church. As a pastor and husband, Dale has witnessed the evils of child sexual abuse within the Christian community. He has witnessed how perpetrators within the church will use and exploit scripture and biblical truths in carrying out their horrors upon little children. He has witnessed time and time again the utter silence of the church in refusing to confront and respond to this grave sin. He has also witnessed the lifelong emotional, physical, and spiritual damage caused by such victimization, and the church's failure to respond with Gospel centered excellence. Far too many have also witnessed such horrors and have responded by simply giving up and walking away in anger and dismay. I would be lying to you if I told you that Dale Ingraham does not get angry and dismayed at how many within the Christian community have turned their backs to this epidemic....however, he has not walked away. Dale Ingraham's love for our great and gracious God and His precious little ones has propelled him to walk towards the church with a message that it has no choice but to hear and embrace. A message that says the days of silence and secrecy surrounding sexual abuse are over, and the days of light and transparency have begun. This is a message that many abuse survivors have been waiting their entire lives to hear. Tragically, it is also a message that many within the church continue to ignore, sometimes vilifying those who bring it…including Dale and Faith Ingraham. "Tear Down These Walls" is a book that clearly brings this powerful Gospel centered message to all who read it. Dale helps us understand the complicated dynamics of sexual abuse within the Church in order that we all may be better equipped in bringing this same message to our respective faith communities. He also provides a comprehensive overview of the myriad of reasons why the Church often prefers darkness and secrecy to light and transparency. Perhaps the most powerful punch of this book is that it is written by one who has not simply studied the subject, but whose life has been so dramatically impacted by all he has seen and experienced.

Supreme Court Justice, William Brandeis once remarked, "Sunshine is the best disinfectant." The only way that we will begin to see transformation within the Christian community in how it understands, confronts, and responds to this dark sin is to bring it light. Ultimately, it is the light of Christ that will shatter the silence and secrecy and bring healing not only to hurting souls, but also to hurting institutions. I praise my friend and my brother for carrying this bright torch into the darkness…you are not alone. There is hope.

Basyle J. Tchividjian

Founder and Executive Director, GRACE

April, 2012

Introduction

"Mr. Gorbachev, Tear down this wall." I remember those words well. I was in my second year at Practical Bible Training School in Johnson City, NY, when President Ronald Reagan said them. I remember the feeling of pride in my country and my president. I was inspired by his courage and determination to face the evils of our day and to dedicate his life to change the evils that faced his presidency and our nation.

The Berlin Wall had stood for many years and was much more than just a symbol of oppression. It divided families, institutions, economics, countries and a way of life. On one side was light, truth, freedom, and the ability to grow; on the other darkness, deceit, oppression and stagnation. It is hard to describe the feeling of excitement we had as we sat glued to the TV watching the crowds gather on both sides of the wall, with each person testing the resolve of the Soviet Union's grip on power, and its decades' long isolation from the rest of the world.

There is a wall, still standing today, that is far greater and more menacing than the Berlin Wall, and it is not the making of some evil empire. It is the making of many in the church. It is not a wall of concrete and steel but it is a wall of silence and secrecy. It is not guarded by soldiers with guns--it is guarded by church leaders with Bibles. Those who dare to climb over this wall are not shot. They are shamed and betrayed by the very ones who should be protecting them.

What is this wall and why was it built? It is a partition that has been long in the making and was built to hide one of the greatest evils in our world, the raping and molesting of children to satisfy a perverted lust in the hearts of many offenders. Sadly, many of our church leaders continue the tradition of maintaining and protecting this wall that conceals the sexual abuse of children from the efforts of those who are trying to tear it down. Keeping the Wall of silence and secrecy allows them to avoid dealing with the sin and the aftermath of the abuse.

Jude 1: 4 says that "For certain individuals whose condemnation was written about long ago have secretly slipped in among you. They are ungodly people, who pervert the grace of our God into a license for immorality ..." (NIV) God was warning the church nearly 2000 years ago, that unscrupulous people were sneaking into the church without being noticed. What does Jude mean by saying they were unnoticed? Surely people saw them physically and noticed that they were there. Jude was saying that their evil intent and motives were unnoticed. In other words, what they were intending to do to the unsuspecting people, was going unnoticed. These deceivers believed that the grace of God gave them the right or license to take sexual advantage of others.

Bill Anderson in his book, *When Sexual Abuse Comes to Church*, tells of a certain church where over sixty children were molested by two older boys who were helping out in the children's ministry. Everyone knew the offending boys were there but they had no idea what was happening under their oversight in the children's ministry. Who would think that someone would come to a church community with such an evil intent? Yet that is what God warned Christians about so long ago in Jude 1:4.

Predators go where they can find prey, and all too often it is in the church. Like the Berlin Wall, this wall of secrecy was built and remains in place primarily for two reasons: to keep some people in and to keep other people out. Religious organizations need this Wall to keep the sin hidden, without it the sin is exposed to the public. The difference between the Berlin Wall and the 'Wall of Silence' is that the Berlin Wall was obvious and visible. This 'wall of silence', on the other hand, is subtle and invisible. The Berlin Wall surrounded a city but the Wall of Silence surrounds a sin.

It is time to challenge Christians everywhere to: "Tear Down This Wall!"

1
The Sin

My wife, Faith, and I founded a not for profit organization in 2008 called "Speaking Truth in Love Ministries" to deal with the issue of sexual abuse in the church today. Early on in building this ministry we realized that although we were both active in church and had attended Christian schools and graduated from Bible College, we had received no teaching on sexual abuse or the extent of its undeniable presence in our society and our churches.

Faith was painfully aware of this issue, since she was a survivor of sexual abuse at the hand of her father, who was a pastor at the time. This pastor raped and molested his daughter from the age of 10 until almost 18 years old. For the most part, I was unaware of the issue of sexual abuse. Both Faith and I had many misconceptions and a great deal of ignorance about this subject.

My recollections of the subject of sexual abuse being addressed were within newspaper articles or radio and TV news broadcasts. These reports mentioned that someone had been raped, usually by a stranger. This media information led me to assume that most sexual assaults are committed by strangers. We have since learned that nothing could be further from the truth. When a person is sexually assaulted, it is most often by someone that they know and is usually someone who is in a position of authority over them. It may be an older family member, a babysitter, a youth leader, a pastor, a deacon, a daycare worker, a boss at work, a scout leader, or the like. It is someone, who by virtue of their relationship or connection, has an advantage over another person and chooses to use that advantage to gratify their desire for sexual pleasure as well as their desire for power and control over that individual.

The statistics show that one in three girls and one in six boys will be raped or molested by the time they are 18 years old. Over the years, when we have quoted these statistics, we have been met with a variety of responses, from 'unbelievable' to 'denial'. For example, several years ago, I was talking with an individual from a Christian ministry and shared our vision for dealing with this difficult issue. He was polite and patient with me, but when I mentioned the statistics, his tone changed and he said that those figures were way too high. He then asked what my source was. I mentioned the resources where we obtained this information. We ended our conversation on a positive note and went our separate ways. Later, in checking the website of the organization that this individual represented, we noticed that they had the identical statistics that I had shared with him during our conversation. This is an example of how one can be unaware about the magnitude of sexual abuse even though they are surrounded by the evidence.

I just read an article in our local paper last week about some educational material that a group from Albany, NY was sending to libraries in New York State in order to teach people about the issues and dangers concerning sexual abuse. In the article, an FBI statistic estimates that 25% of all children in the United States have been sexually abused.

A couple of years ago Faith and I met with a missionary couple who are assigned to work in the United States. When we shared the statistics with them, at first they were shocked, but after thinking about it for a few minutes they stated that sexual assault among the people they work with, might be nearly 100% of the girls!

Christians in America: It is time for us all to wake up and stop the denial. We must take our heads out of the sand. For too long we have said that this evil only happens outside of "our" church. As referenced earlier in the Introduction, shortly after taking on a new church, Bill Anderson found himself in the middle of a pastor's worst nightmare. Over sixty children had been sexually molested in the nursery by two older boys. Even as the facts were coming out about the abuse it was hard for many to believe it actually happened in their church. Pastor Anderson shared that one woman in particular, would raise her hand during the informational meetings and say "This didn't really happen in our church, did it?" Anderson stated, "It was overwhelming to think of children being raped, sodomized, forced into oral sex, beaten and threatened right around the corner from where she was singing hymns and reading her Bible." Bill Anderson, *When Child Abuse Comes to Church*. P.55

I am the pastor of an independent Baptist church, and even though I knew my father-in-law, who was also a Baptist pastor, was an abuser, I still thought that sexual abuse was primarily an issue in other denominations or society in general, but not in ours.

We, as Christians, are good at blaming others for the evils of this world and yet we are not willing to examine our own backyard. We often forget that God says in II Chronicles 7:14 "if My people who are called by My name will humble themselves, and pray and seek My face, and turn from their wicked ways, then I will hear from heaven, and will forgive their sin and heal their land." (NKJV) So often we blame an ungodly world for the problems in society but God seems to put blame on His children, who refuse to turn from "their wicked ways."

This is not a problem of one denomination or another. It is a huge moral and ethical issue; it is a sin issue. It runs across the board--regardless of denomination. It is in the church and it is outside the church, so much so that Bill Anderson says, "The sexual abuse of children is becoming a tragic epidemic in our country." Bill Anderson, *When Child Abuse Comes to Church* p 9

The primary focus of 'Speaking Truth in Love Ministries' is to deal first with this sin, within the church, because it seems unreasonable to think that we can have a meaningful impact in the world until this sin is dealt with in our own midst.

We must take the time to examine the impact of this sin on our churches. (The impact on victims and others will be addressed in later chapters.) I realize that because of the unpleasant nature of this subject that many Christians will be tempted to turn away from what I am trying to share in this book, but I am asking you to consider these issues with an open mind. If these statistics on sexual abuse are anywhere near correct, we must each consider: what are the ramifications for the church? This sin is so widespread that Bill Anderson cautions, "What this means for the churches is that none can expect to remain unaffected by the problem." Bill Anderson, *When Child Abuse Comes to Church,* p. 9

Jesus said in Luke 17:2 that it was better for a millstone to be hung around a person's neck and thrown into the sea than that he should offend one of these little ones. What is Jesus talking about in this verse? He obviously is not talking about proper healthy discipline. He is clearly talking about abuse. Whether it is physical, emotional, spiritual or sexual abuse, Jesus is outraged at the thought of someone offending a child and pronounces "Woe" upon them. I don't know exactly what Christ has in mind, but when He deals with all those who rape and molest children, it will no doubt be a terrifying event.

When considering the consequences of this sin on the church, we must consider the heart and mind of God on the subject. I doubt that there has ever been a pastor who did not pray for God's blessing on their church and ministry, but how can God possibly bless His church when it stubbornly refuses to deal with this gross moral depravity.

Let's compare the present state of the church, to Israel in the Old Testament. In Joshua chapter 7, we find Israel in a great dilemma. God has brought them, under Joshua's leadership, into the 'Promised Land' and as they prepare for their first battle against the wicked city of Jericho, God warns them not to touch the 'accursed thing'. The city was so evil that He wanted everything destroyed. But one of the Jews, by the name of Achan, took some of the accursed items and buried them beneath his tent. Achan took something that was not his and that God never intended him to have, much like the offenders in Luke 17:2 and those, who believe they have a license to commit immorality, that God mentions in Jude 1:4.

From a statistical point of view, beneath every church may be buried 'The accursed thing'. Professing believers in Christ, who attend churches across the country and who reach out and take what is not theirs and then bury it where no one sees, is unfortunately becoming a daily reality. God not only removed His blessing from Achan, but Israel was completely defeated in their next battle against Ai, even though it was a much smaller city and it looked like an easy conquest. Achan's sin caused great pain for his family, and cost the lives of thirty six soldiers and eventually his own life. It was not until Joshua and Israel, as a nation, dealt with Achan's sin, that God could once again bless His people.

While there are some signs of revival in different places around the world, most of the church languishes in frustration and fruitlessness. Child sexual abuse is not the only reason for this, but for sure, it is one of the major ones. Proverbs 28:13 advises that "He who covers his sin will not prosper, but whoever confesses and forsakes them will have mercy." We, the church, want God's mercy and blessing but are we willing to confess and forsake this glaring sin?

When we started our ministry, we thought that we were the only ones doing this kind of work, since then we have found dozens of other ministries doing similar things. One of them is an organization called GRACE, founded by Professor Basyle "Boz" Tchividjian, one of Billy Graham's grandsons and a law professor at Liberty University School of Law in Lynchburg, Virginia. GRACE was asked by a major missionary organization to do an independent investigation of one of their boarding schools in Africa, where allegations of sexual abuse had been made. What GRACE discovered was shocking to say the least. Not only had there been extensive sexual abuse but it had been covered up or ignored by some of the former leadership of the mission. Soon after the investigation, Professor Tchividjian stated that "sexual abuse on the mission field is at an epidemic proportion." When Christians take an honest look at the condition of our churches and mission's programs, we must be sickened at the reality that many of the ones supposedly sent by God to care for the sheep are in fact destroying them. If you doubt this, there are plenty of abuse survivor websites that you can visit and read the stories of pain and suffering caused by the very ones that were sent to care for these children. Also, the film, "All God's Children," follows the stories of abuse from a missionary boarding school in Momau, Africa. Every Christian needs to see this film.

There is the case of Christa Brown who, as a teenager, was raped and molested by the youth pastor. As a young girl, all she wanted to do was to serve the Lord and be a missionary. Her whole world changed after she was sexually assaulted by the youth pastor, she couldn't understand why he would do this to her. When she told the music minister what happened to her, he told her not to tell anyone. She remained silent and kept what had happened to her concealed inside. It was some years later, when she was concerned that this youth pastor might be molesting others, that she came forward with her story. She went back to the church where she had grown up, to tell them her concern and to see if they would help her to expose his sin. To her surprise, no one would help her--they wanted her to be quiet because they were afraid that she would embarrass the entire church. The music minister, who she had told about the abuse, simply would not back up her story. The pain of being rejected by her home church was unbearable. Christa wanted to protect other children from the person who had raped her.

No one at her church ever said that they were sorry for what she had been through, instead she felt rejected and very alone. Is it any wonder why God doesn't bless the Church?

In I Samuel 4 we read a sad story about an old man, by the name of Eli, who was a priest in Israel at the time. He had two sons, Hophni and Phinehas, who were also priests, and who were very wicked. When Israel was invaded by one of her enemies, they took the Ark of the Covenant with them to the battle. Because of their great evil, God allowed Israel to be defeated, Hophni and Phinehas to be killed and the Ark to be taken. Phineas' wife was giving birth when she got the bad news. She named the child 'Ichabod', which means the 'Glory of the Lord is departed'. Has the glory of God departed from our churches today?

Faith and I were in Ohio to meet with Tex Reardon, who was the executive director for Ruth Graham and Friends Ministry. While we were there, a woman shared her story of sexual assault with us. When this woman finally had the courage to share her assault account with the church, they immediately rejected her and refused to believe that her father would ever do something like that to her. She recounted to us that the pain that she felt from the way the church treated her, was like being raped all over again.

The initial sin is the offender's, but by protecting the offender and rejecting the victim, their sin also becomes the church's sin. Consider the following passage: Proverbs 1:15 "He who justifies the wicked and he who condemns the just both of them alike are an abomination to the Lord." When believers protect offenders from the law, they are justifying their evil deeds and when they reject the cries of the abused, they are in effect, condemning them. We have all heard of "blind spots" in people's lives. They are problem areas that for whatever reason are not seen by the individual. In many cases, those who know the person can see them, but the person with the problem doesn't see them. When it comes to the sin of child sexual abuse, it would appear that the church has a blind spot. How is it that we can get so much right such as, doctrine, good works, the gospel, etc. and yet miss such a glaring sin? The world sees it, the victims see it, and the advocates for victims see it, so why doesn't the church as a whole see it? It is like Christians are blind to what is happening all around them.

Too often, when ministries try to confront the issue of sexual abuse, it is only to tell the victim that they need to forgive and move on with their life and that the pain they feel is because they have not forgiven the offender. There is a need to tell the whole truth about what God's Word has to say about sin and forgiveness. We must begin holding offenders accountable and teach that forgiveness does not mean that the offender is protected or exempted from the consequences of their sin.

One of the ways we illustrate this truth is the example of someone being run over by a drunk driver, and they are in the hospital with multiple broken bones and internal injuries. They can forgive the driver that hit them, but their injuries are not going to heal by the forgiveness process. They need medical care and time for their wounds to heal and some injuries may leave permanent damage that can never be repaired, outside of a miracle from God's hand. The same is true for the emotional and spiritual injuries that are suffered, by one who has been sexually abused. They can forgive their offender, but their injuries will still take time to heal and some wounds may be permanent. Similarly, the forgiveness of the victim does not eliminate the consequences to the offender. The drunk driver who hits a person will have to pay for the injuries he caused, face criminal charges and will likely lose his license to drive. The person who has sexually abused another person still needs to face the consequences of their sin regardless of whether their victims have forgiven them. They need to pay for the injuries they have caused, face criminal charges and lose the privilege of being around those who are vulnerable. It is time for the Body of Christ to speak the whole truth about this sin.

2
The Victims

In this chapter I want to discuss how the sin of sexual assault impacts the victim. We hear so many stories of how the church is so concerned for the offender, because they have been such a "good" church member or such a "wonderful" pastor--and they don't want them to suffer in prison, or whatever. But, the important question is: What about the victim? Who gives them a voice? While I have never experienced physical or sexual abuse and therefore can never truly know their pain or suffering, I have witnessed the devastation it leaves behind, in Faith's life and in the many lives of those I have come to know. In the book *By Silence Betrayed* author John Crewson writes about a horrific story of abuse that took place in a small town in Minnesota. There were many children, who were being raped and molested, by many different adults in the town and as it turned out many of the offenders were parents of the victims.

As the investigation continued, some of the victims began talking about seeing children killed and buried, yet the investigators could find no bodies, but the children were truly terrified, as they would recount the details of the murders. One of the investigators finally concluded, that the children were talking metaphorically about the death of their own souls. Here is what he said: "I think the children were crying out to us in reporting the death of their own inner soul, their own spiritual life and they were screaming to us in a sense of saying, "We are dying here, this is killing us.'" When Faith shares her testimony, she recounts how she died emotionally, not long after her dad began abusing her. Only the victims can truly know the darkness and devastation that begins to take over as their abuser has his way with them.

Until 2005, I was the only one Faith had told about her abuse. Faith recounts that even as a pastor's wife, if someone had asked her if she had ever been sexually abused, she probably would have said no, because the pain and embarrassment was just too great. People often ask: "Why don't they just tell someone?" For most victims, the thought of telling someone is so terrifying that they are unable to do so until much later in life. Bill Anderson said in his book: "In our case, not one of the sixty victims reported the abuse." (Bill Anderson, *When Child Abuse Comes to Church*, p.55) It was not until Faith found out her abuser, now a grandfather, had molested her niece, that she realized her silence was allowing her father, though much older now, to continue to rape and molest. As I mentioned before, we were very ignorant about the complexities of this sin and about the twisted nature of offenders. We thought that Faith was her father's only victim and had hoped and assumed, that he had repented and was a changed person. Although rumors of 'adultery' seemed to pop up now and then, no one seemed compelled to find out the truth behind these unverified reports. In one of the studies that we quote in our material, it was discovered that the average offender had 117 victims. A staggering statistic, if that is true; we can only imagine how easy it is for one offender to destroy a whole family, a church, or a community.

When a child is raped or molested, it causes shock waves that shatter many areas of their life. It is hard for anyone to admit that they have been sexually assaulted, but it is especially hard for boys and men. One male survivor puts it this way "The very hardest part of recovery for me was coming out and saying that I am a sexually abused person. I didn't know until two years ago that men and boys could be raped. We're not supposed to be victims." (Wendy Maltz, *The Sexual Healing Journey*, Pg 51) When a child is sexually assaulted an innocence is stolen that can never be replaced. What does it mean that their innocence was stolen? It is more than something precious being taken away; we are talking about a state of innocence. In a way like Adam and Eve in the garden, they were created without sin. God gave them a command, but there came a day when Eve and Adam both disobeyed. One of the ways that Satan enticed Eve to disobey God and to eat of the tree, was by telling her, that if she ate the fruit that she would be like God, knowing good and evil. Eve may have only heard the "knowing good" and missed the part about "knowing evil." Innocence was more than just, being in a state of goodness, it was the absence of evil.

When Adam and Eve chose to sin, they discovered for the first time what evil was. The Bible tells us that because of Adam and Eve's sin that all mankind is born into sin and need a savior. God made a provision by which mankind could all be saved. He sent His Son to this earth, as a man, so that He could die on a cross and pay the penalty for everyone's sin and rise from the dead the third day. When anyone puts their faith and trust in Christ alone, they are redeemed, their sins are forgiven, and they are in that instant, a child of God.

Victims of sexual assault did not sin, but were viciously sinned against by their offender. When we say, that their innocence was taken away, it is more than something being taken away; for the first time in their life they know what evil is. We live in a wicked world and all too soon children learn what evil is, how sad when someone entrusted with their care or safety, forces that evil upon them.

While I was talking with a person who had suffered abuse, and was sharing about our ministry, I used the term victim in referring to a person who had been abused. She quickly told me that she was a survivor. The term victim was offensive to her. While only someone who has gone through abuse can truly know or feel what they are experiencing, there are some things that we have observed from talking with people who have gone through the experience of sexual assault and from reading their stories. From the books that we have read and the survivors that we have talked to, it seems that a person who has suffered abuse goes through several stages in the healing process.

Victim Stage

The first stage of their healing process is the victim stage. Webster describes someone who is a victim as, "someone who is acted upon and is adversely affected…" as well as "one that is injured, destroyed, sacrificed…" When someone has been raped or molested, the devastation is incalculable. Pain, sadness, guilt, hatred, a loss of self-worth and confusion all come flooding into their life. Again, many people wonder why doesn't the child do something to stop the abuse? In all cases of sexual abuse, the offender has some sort of power over the victim. It can be age, strength, will, money, guilt, intimidation, threats of harming others or any number of other things. There is a long list of ways that sexual offenders exert power over their prey --hence the term 'victim'. Those assaulted in this way feel powerless to help themselves or powerless to escape their offender. Bill Anderson puts it this way; "Children know they cannot withstand the attacks of adults who are always smarter and more powerful, so the only form of defense they know is acquiescence." (Bill Anderson, *When Child Abuse Comes to Church*, Pg 39)

The world, as they knew it, had changed for the worse, and they did not know what the future would hold. Many victims are threatened or told their loved ones will be killed or harmed if they tell. Many of the children at the missionary boarding school that I referred to earlier were told that if they said anything about their abuse, their parents would have to leave the mission field and that the natives would die and go to Hell and it would be their fault! There are many reasons why most victims do not report their abuse. Fear of the unknown, what will happen to them, what will happen to their family or church and so on. Many victims never leave this stage. They remain trapped by fear and shame, never able to truly get on with their lives. They struggle with jobs, relationships and a sense of not being able to cope with life. As a pastor, I have seen many broken relationships, where abuse had played a role in their struggles. People with life controlling issues often have sexual abuse in their background. One victim explains how her abuse impacted her. "The guilt, shame, and confusion were indescribable and agonizing. Didn't God care about her? … She became very angry with God and didn't want to go to church." (Lynn Heitritter &

Jeanette Vought, *Helping Victims of Sexual Abuse*, p. 61) While in the victim stage, it seems to be a constant struggle to keep from drowning. It is a constant cry for help and often involves some form of addiction. It is often characterized by a continual need for counseling and the constant attention of someone else- just to make it through each day. We live in a cruel world. In the animal kingdom the wounded and hurt are abandoned and rejected by their parents and siblings. The same is often true with people when it comes to victims of sexual abuse. What one person's love should a child be able to count on more than any other? If you asked one thousand people that question, most would say their mother. Yet the reality is that many moms reject their children who have been sexually abused and are deeply wounded. To this day Faith's mother refuses to comfort her or allow Faith to discuss the abuse with her. Listen to what this mom has to say, to her daughter. "Mrs. Taylor looked intently at her thirteen-year-old daughter and asked, "How could you do this to me? You took my husband away and you have ruined the family." (*Helping Victims of Sexual Abuse*, P 78)

Faith and I have heard many stories of those who have been rejected and even turned against, because of their experience of sexual assault. Isaiah 59:1-4 recounts Israel's sinful state and that their sinful way of life included the fact that: no one called for justice and that no one made a plea for the truth. They simply ignored the plea of innocent victims. That, so often is happening in homes and churches today. The victim is simply abandoned, by family and the church.

We had a lady come up to us after one of our conferences and thanked us for dealing with the issue of sexual abuse. She went on to share that, years before her children had been molested by the youth pastor. When she and her husband went to the leadership of the church, she said "they practiced shunning . . . they shunned us!" Nothing was done to the youth pastor. No action--all too often is the course of action that many churches take! Many Christians depend on their church leadership to deal with the sexual offender. Unfortunately, in their attempts to take any reasonable action, they so often end up never calling the authorities to report this as a crime. As stated earlier: sexual assault is a crime and it needs to be reported to the legal authorities!

In the book *Invisible Girls,* Dr. Patti Feuereisen tells victims: "the most important thing you can do is simply tell someone, because telling is the beginning of healing." Take a moment and think about what that means. It is vital for a victim to have the opportunity to share openly what they have been through. It gives them validation that they matter and that someone cares enough about them to listen. But what has the church historically done? More often than not when a victim has mustered up enough courage to share their story, the church leadership often tells them that they need to forgive and forget and get on with their life. What is really meant is: "Please don't make a fuss as it could make things difficult for the church, not to mention "us."

When we had the British Petroleum oil spill, in the Gulf of Mexico, in 2010 the CEO kept putting his foot in his mouth. There was great outrage, when he said "I want my life back." Eleven had died in the explosion and millions of gallons of oil had spilled into the gulf and all he could think about was getting his own life back. Well I'm sure that he didn't mean it to sound as bad as it did, but many were deeply offended. When the church tells someone, whose life has been so damaged by sexual abuse, that they can't share their story or report this crime; they are sending the same message "You don't matter, your pain doesn't matter, and the injustice doesn't matter. We just want our life and ministry to be undisturbed."

In I Thessalonians 5:14 we read Paul's exhortation to: ". . . warn those who are unruly, comfort the faint hearted, uphold the weak…" When it comes to the issue of dealing with sexual assault, it seems that we have done almost everything wrong. We protect the offender and silence the victim, under the pretext of not wanting to hurt the cause of Christ. Forcing, telling, or encouraging a victim to keep silent, is like shutting them away in a closet. The silence becomes a cocoon which preserves the child in their present state, never allowing them to heal. Here is how one victim describes it: "Believing that we have to remain silent about something confusing and painful that happened to us can be another form of victimization. 'I had to acknowledge I was a victim before I could see myself as a survivor,' one man said." (*The Sexual Healing Journey*, p. 50) Actually, the sin that really hurts the cause of Christ, is--not dealing with it!

Survivor Stage

The second stage is that of being a survivor. Webster defines "survive" as "to remain alive or in existence." Someone who is a survivor of sexual abuse is someone who gets beyond the victim stage and is able to get on with their life. The pain and damage is still there, but they have found a way to move forward. The individuals are able to hold a good job or establish a career. Their relationships are stable and they can get married and raise their children in a good environment. They are able to bury the past and do not dwell on it.

With the survivor stage, there is healing, but it is apparently only on the surface. It is like knowing someone with cancer and you know they are in pain and not feeling well and yet they are often able to put on a good front when people say to them, "You look well today.", but inside, they are in misery. To the world, and sometimes even to their close friends, the survivor looks well and appears to have it all together, but on the inside it is as though the assault happened yesterday and they often still carry the hurt and anger. "Many survivors of sexual abuse have tremendous anger toward God, their parents, and other Christians who did not understand the deep pain of the abuse they endured." (*Helping Victims of Sexual Abuse*, P 67)

All you have to do is listen to a survivor tell their story and watch the tears come into their eyes or hear the pain, fear, or even hate, that comes into their voice and you recognize that the wounds are still there. My wife, Faith, was a survivor. Faith had gone to college to get her Associates Degree and then to Bible College. This is where we met. Faith has great secretarial skills and is a kind and loving person, but the healing was only superficial. It wasn't until she came forward with her story and we started our ministry to speak out against sexual abuse that the real healing began to take place. I can see every time that she shares her testimony and we have a chance to speak in churches, that she heals a little more each time. I think most victims are in the survivor stage. Statistics show that most women are not ready to talk about their abuse until they are in their mid-40s. If that statistic is true, and if telling their story is the first step to healing, then most women do not experience that healing until later in life.

One lady shared with us that she had been raped when she was in her mid-teens by someone who was a guest speaker at her church. This man was invited to spend the night at their house while he was visiting their church. He took that opportunity to rape her during the night and threatened her that if she told anyone, her father would have to leave the ministry. The next day this monster got up in the pulpit to preach. This same lady told us that she thought for years, that she was going to hell because of what had been done to her. "A single incident of any type of sexual abuse can have lasting damaging effects on a little child" (*Children and Sexual Abuse*, p 7) She had told no one for years that she had been raped and when she was sharing her story with us, she was in her late 40's and had told only her parents and her husband. After hearing Faith's testimony she was able to have the courage to share her own story.

Another difference between a survivor and a victim is that the victim's struggles with life and relationships are obvious to others, although they may have no idea why this person is struggling. The survivor, on the other hand, is able to hide or suppress their difficulties and pain, to the point that when they do eventually share what they have gone through people are shocked because they had no idea. I was watching Mike Huckabee's show one Sunday night and he had a well-known comedian as a guest. I tuned in as the interview was under way and he started talking about his childhood and how a babysitter had repeatedly molested him. I was caught off guard, because it was not what I expected to hear. Many of the people we know personally and publically have been through one or many sexual assaults and yet have kept the secret for many years.

In Ecclesiastes 4:9-10, we read that: "Two are better than one… for if they fall, one will lift up his companion. But woe to him who is alone when he falls for he has no one to help him up." We can conclude that a survivor has found a way to stand. Maybe it was by reaching out to God or to a compassionate person, but somehow they have managed to stand. The person in the victim stage has still not been able to stand. People may be "lending" the hand, but the victim is not able or comfortable enough to accept the help. For many, it simply boils down to a lack of trust.

Christians through the centuries have been comforted by the words in Hebrews 13:5-6, which says "… I will never leave you nor forsake you. So we may boldly say 'The Lord is my helper, I will not fear what man can do to me'." Most people who go through abuse wonder where God was when those awful things were happening to them. I don't think we can truly understand the answer to that question. God is always there, and if we know Him as our Lord and Savior, He promises to never leave us. This world is filled with evil and broken, sinful people. There is a day coming when God will unleash His wrath upon this world and on those who practice evil, but in the meantime, Romans 2:5 says they are "storing up wrath against the day of wrath." To anyone who has gone through abuse, you need to know that God dearly loves you and wants to comfort you and bring healing into your life, but He does not force Himself on you. God may use someone in your life to help bring comfort and hope, but you will have to be willing to receive it.

Victor Stage

The Third stage is victory. I discovered something as I was writing this book that is so obvious, but I had never thought of it before. In Webster's dictionary the word "victor" immediately follows the word "victim." Yes, I know that everyone else probably knew that, but when I saw it, I thought how fitting it was. Webster describes a victor as "one who defeats an enemy." True victory in anyone's life can only be found in Jesus Christ. The victor is one who has found a way to defeat the enemy. For those who have been assaulted, the 'enemy' may be their offender or it may be the memory of the attack, it also could be the shame and rejection that they have had to endure. Whatever or whoever the 'enemy' is, the victor has found a way to break free from its power. They are not held prisoner by hate, fear, shame, or a sense of guilt. The victor is a victim who became a survivor and survivor who eventually broke free from the prison that had enslaved them.

Faith and I have been married for 26 years and as an observer of the struggles she has had over her abuse, I believe that only since coming forward with her story has she truly become a victor. Faith has grown and flourished more in the past five years than in the previous 21 years combined. Being a victor does not mean that you don't feel the pain or have memories that you struggle with. It means that you have faced your enemy and broken its grip over you. Over the years I have counseled people with depression, self-doubt, and a sense of worthlessness. One of the things that have been a great help to these people is when they can reach out and help others. First, the person must deal truthfully with their own issues and then take opportunities to reach out and help others. As I have watched Faith on her healing journey, I have noticed that each time she shares her story of abuse and rejection that she heals a little more. She has discovered that, even though it hurts to speak about her abuse, others are finding help and comfort.

II Corinthians 1:3-4 says "Blessed be the God and Father of our Lord Jesus Christ, the Father of mercies and the God of all comfort, who comforts us in all our tribulation that we may be able to comfort those who are in any trouble, with the same comfort with which we ourselves are comforted by God." One thing that helps a survivor to become a victor is receiving God's comfort and then turning and helping someone else who has gone through abuse.

I saw a commercial the other day where a number of people were shown individually saying the same words: "It happened to me." As I listened to one after the other say the same thing, I knew that they were talking about being sexually assaulted even though it was not mentioned at first. It went on to offer hope and encouragement for those who had gone through such a horrific experience. If God has helped you to get through abuse, then I believe that God wants you to help someone else.

In the old Dr. Seuss classic *"Horton Hears a Who,"* Horton, the elephant, hears a faint sound coming from a clover blossom. Upon further inspection he discovers that there is a tiny, tiny city on the clover blossom. When his protective instincts kick in, it raises the curiosity and ire of the other creatures of the jungle. Convinced that he is crazy, they decide, for his own good, that they need to destroy the clover blossom and the problem will go away. Only Horton, with his keen hearing, could hear the voice of the mayor of the tiny city. When Horton realized what was about to happen, he told the mayor to get all the town's people together and make as much noise as possible, in the hopes that the other animals would finally be able to hear them too.

The mayor frantically warns the people of the coming danger and convinces them to start yelling as loud as they can. At first, Horton's friends could hear nothing and continued with their plans to destroy the clover blossom. In the meantime, the people, in the tiny city of Whoville, were making all kinds of noise and they started to chant a simple chant together. As all the people of the city joined together, the chant got louder "We are here, we are here, we are here." Finally, the chant grew loud enough to break through the invisible barrier of silence and the doubters were able to hear the cry for help from the city.

Even though the existence and number of victims of sexual abuse is staggering, we still have many doubters. The doubters include many, if not most, church leaders, as well as many of the people in the pews. We need your voice saying: "we are here" to be heard loud and clear, before the church will truly be awakened and the wall of secrecy and silence that surrounds this sin will finally come down. I know that I am using a child's story to try and illustrate something that is tragically serious, but like Horton, there are people who have heard the cries of those who have suffered sexual assault in the church and they are trying to convince a skeptical church leadership that Christians need to deal with this heinous sin. We need you as the victims of these crimes to stand and let the doubters know that you really are here.

3
The Offender

Repentance and the Offender

Webster defines "offend" as to transgress a moral law..., to cause pain, hurt..." Offenders come in all shapes and sizes; they come from all walks of life and can be either male or female. "Child abusers can be rich or poor, smart or stupid, boorish or charming, failed or successful, black or white, or any other skin color, for that matter. Even some of the judges, prosecutors, police officers and social workers whose job it is to put child molesters behind bars and to protect their victims, have been convicted of molesting children." (John Crewdson, *By Silence Betrayed* p. 55) Someone who rapes or molests another person, not only causes pain and hurt, but they break God's law as well as the law of the land. Sexual assault is a criminal offence! An offender must pay the consequences of his deeds.

My experience with offenders comes from the time that I have known Faith's dad, from books that we have read on the subject, from the many heartbreaking stories that victims have shared, as well as from people I have known personally, who were arrested for their crimes. The question is: Can a sexual offender repent of their sin? The answer is, yes. Can they be forgiven? The answer is, yes. Is it possible for them to change? The initial answer would be: "with God all things are possible" Matthew 10:27. However, I think that truly repentant offenders are very rare, even amongst professing Christians. Dad could cry big crocodile tears at the drop of a hat. It was obvious that his sorrow was not over the pain he had caused his victims. His grief was over the fact that he got caught and self-pity over facing the consequences of his actions.

Second Corinthians 7:10 reminds us that: "godly sorrow produces repentance." Unfortunately, statistics and experience seem to verify that the sexual offender's sorrow is usually a self-serving sorrow. It is not that they are all of a sudden concerned for their victims and the harm they have done to them. The typical offender is focused on their own issues. They worry about money, jail, embarrassment, their own careers and even their ministries. According to this verse, if the sorrow is a godly sorrow, it will bring about a true repentance. So if an offender does not repent and turn from their sin to God and demonstrate that, by changing their behavior and accepting the consequences of their sin, then we must conclude, that it was not godly sorrow.

Offenders will often claim they were crazy or that they had an illness, as a way to excuse their behavior. Bill Anderson contests this by suggesting in his book that this is a myth: **"One myth about sex abusers is that they are insane...* They know what they are doing is wrong. That is why they go to such lengths to keep it secret." (Bill Anderson,** *When child Abuse Comes to Church***, pp 52-53)** In actuality, when an offender makes a practice of raping and molesting one child, they develop "skills" that help them to go from one victim to another, without getting caught. For many offenders, it is as much about power and control as it is about sex.

Somehow, most offenders convince their victims not to tell anyone. Some of the reasons that victims have given for not telling about their sexual assault are: they were told that their parents would have to leave the ministry; they were told that people would go to hell; they were threatened with death or pain; their family members would be killed; they were told their sisters would be raped; they were told it was God's will; they were told that they were bad and that they deserved it, and so on. Bill Anderson mentions in his book, that children would even deny that they had been sexually assaulted, because they were afraid. "Victims also lie, but they do it out of fear. They generally do not lie about who abused them, or about the kinds of things that have been done to them. They simply deny the fact that they have been abused because they have been threatened or are extremely afraid." (Bill Anderson, *when child Abuse Comes to Church*, Pg 53)

One of the ways that offenders keep victims silent is through threats. One woman who shared her story said that her father put a gun to her brother's head and told her, that if she ever told anyone that he would kill her brother and mother and then himself and leave her alive and it would be her fault. Perpetrators threaten to kill or injure the victim or their loved ones. In other cases they threaten that bad things will happen to their family, like the loss of their job, ministry, reputation and so forth. Another way that offenders will keep their victims from talking is to blame them and say it was their fault; it was the way that they dressed or the way that they acted. Perpetrators of sexual assault are skilled liars and manipulators. They usually succeed in convincing their victims to be quiet. The victims feel that they are guilty and that they have done something wrong and so they lock themselves in a virtual prison, never telling anyone what happened. This was the experience of the woman that I mentioned earlier who thought for years that she was going to hell for what someone else had done to her. When an offender uses these "skills" to keep their victims isolated and in check, you can be sure that it is not the first time they have done this and it means that they are well practiced.

Patrick Crough, who is a retired investigator and author, tells parents how to keep the communication lines open with their children, in order to protect them. "Remember one of the predator's most effective tools is manipulating a child into silence… Parents can eliminate this tool by drawing out their children every day, to find out who is treating them special." (Patrick Crough, *Serpents Among Us*, Pg. 147)

Another way that sexual perpetrators keep their victims in subjection is to tell them that they are worthless and that no one loves them and that this is happening to them because they are bad. One woman who shared her story with us at a conference we did in Albany, NY said that, after years of sexual abuse by her father that she felt so dirty and filthy that she actually thought she smelled to others. Precious children are being beaten verbally into submission. They are being lied to and constantly deceived in order that very evil people can have their own gratifications. I can see my father-in law with his arrogant attitude and that cocky look on his face as he proclaims his own goodness and hides behind God's Grace to excuse his horrible deeds on children. I doubt he will be so smug when he finally stands before God to account for his deeds. Although he led Faith to Christ when she was five, he began to rape and molest her when she was nine or ten, until she was around eighteen years of age. This father and pastor continued to preach in the pulpit and to serve communion with un-confessed sin in his heart. Faith's father never once asked for her forgiveness, which means that he was not right with God during most of the time that he was in the ministry. I realize that a Christian can fall back into sin and that they may battle some sins their whole life. We have many examples of this in the Bible, such as David, Solomon, and others. But when an offender lives this pattern for much of his or her life without remorse or repentance, we must conclude that God does not dwell in them. Hebrews 12:8 says; "But if you are without chastening, of which all are partakers then are you bastards and not sons." There are many in the church who claim to be Christians, but their life doesn't back up their claim. When someone, who claims to be a Christian, sins and does not experience God's chastening hand, God says he is an illegitimate child. First John 3:6 says "Whoever abides in Him does not sin. Whoever sins has neither seen Him nor known Him." God already mentioned earlier in John that if anyone says he is without sin, he is a liar. The battle against sin is a constant battle. That is why Paul reminds Christians in Ephesians 6 to put on the whole armor of God. When someone's life has this continual pattern of sin and there is no repentance and it appears that God does not chasten them, it means they are not one of His children. We can wrestle with this issue our whole life, but only God knows for sure who has truly repented of their sin and who has fully put their trust in Christ.

There are a number of things that must happen in order to consider the possibility that an offender is truly repentant. There must be: Confession, repentance, restitution, accepting of the consequences, and an aim to try to stop the spread of this sin. In the following section, I am going to examine each one of these topics as it relates to offenders.

Confession and the Offender

Confession means more than just admitting to doing something wrong. It means agreeing with God about our sin. When dad molested one of Faith's nieces, not only did Faith come forward with her story, but we also learned about other victims. There were Christians at the time who said that dad didn't have to deal with previous victims because they were in the past. If a sin has not been confessed and dealt with, it doesn't matter if it was fifty years ago, as far as God is concerned it may as well have been yesterday. Sin can only be forgiven and put behind someone when it has been confessed and dealt with. The offender must: 1. Confess to God, 2. Confess to those he has sinned against, and 3. Since this is a crime, confess it to the law. Anything less is not a true confession, it is only an attempt to mitigate the trouble that they find themselves in. As to our confession before God, Psalm 51 describes David's confession of his sins and is a good model of what a repentant person should do. He weeps continually over his sin; he openly confesses his sin to the world; he makes no excuses for his sin and he truly desires a right relationship with the Lord.

As to confession to those who have been sinned against, Jesus told his listeners in Matthew 5:23-24 that if they brought a gift to the altar and remembered that someone had something against them, they were to go and make it right first and then come bring their gift. The teaching that we glean from this passage is that an offender cannot be right with God until he or she has made things right with those they have sinned against. That may seem like an impossible mountain to climb, but it is a mountain of the offender's own making.

It is mandatory that those who commit sexual offenses realize that they have committed criminal acts. Part of the confession process means that offenders need to confess their crimes to the authorities as well. As to confessing to the authorities, God makes it very clear in Romans 13 that we are to be subject to the law, "for he is God's minister to execute wrath upon those who do evil."

Religion and the Offender

It may seem like a very strange statement, but many offenders are religious. Every Christian needs to see the documentary film "All God's Children." It is a documentary about a missionary boarding School in Mamou, Africa in the 1950's to 1970's. A lady in our church attended the school and witnessed the rampant sexual and physical abuse of the children by some of the missionaries who were supposed to be caring for them. I watched that film with tears as I listened to one lady who had been molested, tell her story. She said for years, that whenever she would think of God she would only see the face of her offender. When someone is sexually assaulted by a religious person, they learn to equate God with that person. There was a program on television a few years ago that told the story of a man who abducted a girl and kept her as a sex slave for a number of years, before he was found out and arrested. The girl told investigators that after he would rape her, he would read the Bible to her! Remember that 'religious' does not mean Godly.

The children at the boarding school described sitting in chapel and being told to sing the hymns and memorize the verses by the same ones who were raping, molesting, and beating them. Some of the missionaries serving at the school had no idea of the sexual assaults and physical abuse that was happening there, but some did know and did little or nothing to stop it. Not all of the offenders were men. To most Christians this school would appear to be the model missionary school. They had the children in chapel every day and they were singing and memorizing verses, but what was happening in secret was vile indeed. The religious offenders who were at this school were like the Pharisees of Jesus' day. Jesus said in Matthew 23:27 "Woe to you, scribes and Pharisees, hypocrites! For you are like whitewashed tombs which indeed appear beautiful on the outside, but inside are full of dead men's bones and all uncleanness." Wow, what powerful words and what a picture of the "religious" offender. Yes, I often wonder how many people have turned away from God because of people like my father-in-law and the missionaries at this boarding school.

Offenders do not just stop what they are doing. Even offenders, who appear to be repentant and accept the consequences of their sin and do everything expected of them to make things right, should never be around children. This is part of the consequences of their actions. For example, there was a story in our local paper this past summer about a man in his 80's who was arrested for molesting a child. A month or two later, there was someone in their 90's arrested for the same thing. Believe it or not, that same year, there was a story about a man, who was 100 years old, who was being released from prison after serving his sentence for child sexual abuse! His family wanted nothing to do with him. He said he wanted to see his grandchildren and great-grandchildren and tell them he had done nothing wrong. He was rearrested a short time later.

There are a few ministries that are trying to help sexual offenders to break the cycle of harmful abuse. These are much-needed ministries and as it happens, some of them are led by people who were offenders. If there is any hope of an offender turning their life around, they must not only break the cycle of sin, but they must come full circle in their transformation process. In other words, it is not just enough to stop the sin of assaulting people sexually, but they must begin doing what is right. If a rehabilitation program focuses only on stopping a particular behavior it is destined to have little success.

In Ephesians 4:28, we can read what Paul told those in the Ephesian church: "Let him that stole, steal no longer, but rather let him labor, working with his hands what is good, that he may have something to give him who has need." That is what it means to come full circle. So how would an offender come full circle? It would be a long journey for sure, but I think that the end of that journey would be helping other offenders to break the cycle of sin and be a help in changing their lives.

Let me close this section with two examples from my experience, one is about an offender who may be truly repentant and the other one is about someone who obviously is not. Both of these men were pastors and they are people I knew personally. The first man had molested two boys from his church. When he was caught and charged with the crime, he knew that he had done more than what he was being charged with. He knew that to be truly right with God he needed to make a full confession. He told me later that the judge called him a fool for confessing to the rest. When I met him at his home before his sentencing, he was working on a curriculum for offenders. He had a desire to do something that would help stop this sin and bring about change in an offender's life. I left his house believing that he was repentant and that someday God would be able to use him as a force for good against this evil. He was sentenced to twelve years in prison. Time will tell if he was sincere.

The other man was a pastor who molested a young girl. Two weeks later after confessing the deed to the girl's father, he was in another church singing in their choir! He had no shame at all. When I met with this person, I will never forget when I entered his house, he was sitting on the couch with an open Bible next to him. As we walked in, he put his hand on the Bible and started talking about all the things God had been teaching him! He wanted us to believe that he was already right with God and therefore, no consequences were necessary. When another group of believers met with him, to discern if he was truly repentant, they stressed he would never be able to minister to women or children again, but maybe if he got his life right, he might have a ministry to men. His response was that, he was not ready to be a 'homosexual'. At first when I heard that, I thought it was simply another foolish statement that he had made. After I thought about it, I realized it was much more than that.

The statement was a revelation of this man's thought processes. When he said "I am not ready to be a homosexual", the statement showed how he used his pastoral ministry to gain access to victims. Ministry for this pastor was about having sex with children, not preaching the gospel. It was about himself, not others; it was about sin, not righteousness. Ministry meant having a steady stream of potential victims, nothing more. If a ministry with men meant that he would have to be a homosexual, what else could we conclude than that a ministry that included women and children would be one where he was having sexual contact with them? This is the mindset of a monster not a minister; it is the mind of someone who is evil. If he was concerned about Christian ministry, he would be willing to do the things necessary to get his life right with God and keep from harming others.

Offenders not only have evil intent, but they can and do strike quickly and at times when no one would think it was possible that something could happen. In his book *The Serpents Among Us,* Patrick Crough recounts one of the cases he worked on where an offender needed only minutes with two children to do the unthinkable. "This case also epitomizes just how quickly the undetected child predator can strike. Without warning, he finally lunges to destroy and devour his prey. Within a twenty-minute time frame, he sexually assaulted one little girl in front of another and even brazenly memorialized the event on camera, while one of their mothers was right upstairs visiting with two other women." (Patrick Crough, *The Serpents Among Us*, pg 184)

In most cases, offenders fall into this latter category, not the first-meaning that they are not repentant. Hopefully those who are repentant can find the help they need, so that once they have served the sentence for their crime they can break the cycle of sin and help other offenders do the same. Based on his many years of experience with investigating sex abuse cases, Patrick Crough has put together a list of warning signs that someone may be getting too close to your children.

CAUTION FLAGS

1. Offers of Assistance

2. Great Personal Investment

3. Seeking Constant Contact

4. Professionals seeking alone time with your child outside of their normal role

5. Teenage boys providing child care

6. Men making your life very convenient.

7. Possessiveness

8. Solo travel

9. Interest in pornography

10. Excessive compliments

(Patrick Crough, *Serpents Among Us*, Pp. 301-303)

4
The Enablers

Webster says that to 'enable' means to "Provide with the means and opportunity." Most enablers probably do not think of themselves as enablers. As unpleasant as it is to consider, the enablers are the ones who allow the offender to continue their evil practices. Although the original sin is done by the offenders, the question is: why are they seldom caught and how can they manage to go from one victim to another without the unsuspecting public finding out? It is because of a variety of reasons, but one of them, is because of the presence and subtle assistance of an enabler. To enable a predator, to continue preying on children, is in itself a sin and in most cases is a crime.

We'll divide enablers into two categories: direct enablers and indirect enablers. By direct enabler I mean those people who get involved in the situation. They take action. They make phone calls, they write letters. They talk with people. They get lawyers and others involved. They do all this in an effort to minimize the consequences for the offender. The indirect enabler is one who finds out what has happened or suspects what has happened and does nothing. Both will answer to God for their deeds. James 4:17 says "Therefore, to him who knows to do good and does not do it, to him it is sin."

Direct Enablers

Direct enablers are motivated by a number of different things. I will deal with three motivational factors that I have witnessed.

The first motivation is self-preservation. Whenever a case of sexual abuse becomes known, there are always people who think: "How is this going to affect me or my organization?" There is nothing wrong with the question itself, but when a person, for the sake of self-preservation, decides to enable the offender, they become part of the crime. An example of personal preservation might be a family member of the offender, who believes there may be negative financial consequences such as a law suit, or loss of income from the offender's job. These individuals take steps to protect the offender, thereby protecting themselves.

If the assault has not yet been reported to the law, they may contact the victim or their family and urge them not to report it, because it will cause more pain for the victim and embarrass the family. When the victim and the offender are in the same family, all too often, the child has no advocate, because the ones who should be protecting the child decide that their personal preservation is more important than the child's safety or justice. We saw this in one case where the grandmother to the victim was more concerned about keeping her home and her "dignity". She encouraged her husband to get a lawyer and to say that the abuse was the granddaughter's fault.

Then there is organizational preservation. This is what happens in churches and other organizations where sexual abuse takes place. When it is discovered everyone goes into damage control mode. In the two earlier cases, where I mentioned the abuse at the mission boarding schools, some of the leaders ignored and even covered up the abuse so that the organization's image wouldn't be hurt or tarnished. What often happens in these cases is that because the offender is deemed to be valuable to the organization or the church, they simply move them someplace else and hope the situation will be forgotten. We are reminded of the Scripture passage in Luke 12:2 that states: "For there is nothing covered that will not be revealed, nor hidden that will not be known." Numbers 32:23 "…be sure your sin will find you out."

Some direct enablers are motivated by a misguided desire to "help." They think the best thing is to get this situation over as quickly as possible. They think that the fewer people who know about this, the better, and that this should be kept "in house." "Don't let the authorities know because it will be too traumatic for the victim," The more something is buried the more pain it causes in the end and the more damage that is done. It is like toxic waste that is dumped and buried illegally, it never goes away. Once abuse has occurred, there is no painless solution. It must be fully dealt with for the victim to find lasting healing. The "helper enabler" hurts the victim, by wanting a quick resolution, because it usually means that they can't tell anyone else about what has happened to them. This reinforces what the offender has been saying, "don't tell anyone." This further demoralizes the victim. The "helper enabler" is not helping the offender either. Would you let your friend or family member drive while they are drunk? Most of us would not, because we don't want them to get hurt or to hurt anyone else. Protecting an offender allows them to continue in their sin and perhaps on the road to Hell. In the end the enabler helps no one. They only allow the abuse to continue.

There is also the enabler who has a misguided affection for the offender. It may be a woman who wants the affection of someone, who is an offender. This desire is so strong that she would put her own children in danger if it means that she can be with this person. We knew a woman who clearly had a misguided affection for the offender. The offender was married, but when she would see him at church, she would kiss him on the lips and rub his stomach in greeting him. When he was in the hospital she pushed past his wife, to stand at the head of his bed, and laughed when the nurses thought she was his wife. When she learned he had molested his granddaughter, she tried to keep the church from finding out the truth. When the church broke off fellowship and refused to let him continue leading a Bible study, she worked behind the scenes to have him return. She showed no concern for his victims or even her own grandchildren who had been exposed to him. After she knew the truth about what he had done and the years that he had raped and molested his victims, she proudly raised her hand in church one Sunday and said that he was a wonderful pastor. As outrageous as this behavior is, it is not uncommon.

We hear many stories of single moms with boyfriends. For the offender, this is the perfect scenario. The single mom is usually very needy and often has children, who need a father. The sexual predator will use this relationship to get access to the children. In many cases the mom is working and the boyfriend has complete control of the children while she is gone. The children become trapped in their own home.

Hosea 2:5 says "for their mother has played the harlot; she who conceived them has behaved shamefully, for she said, 'I will go after my lovers, who give me my bread and my water…'

Indirect Enablers

Indirect enablers are those who hear about abuse but do nothing at all. They don't want to talk about it. They want to pretend that it didn't happen or that it will just go away. After all, those things happened in the past and there is nothing that can be done about it now. We have seen cases where indirect enablers have been victims of abuse themselves and feel powerless to change things. Fear, shame, and indifference seem to be the motivating factors for these enablers. When incest occurs within the home, many mothers deny its existence. In the book "Surviving the Secret," there is an account of a study of 112 mothers: "researchers found that although they denied incest occurring, all the mothers were aware of it and of the collusive role they played." These mothers didn't want to talk about the abuse. They just wanted to pretend that it didn't happen or that it would just go away. After all, those things happen and there's nothing much a person can do about it. They fear the wrath and anger of the sexual abuser; they fear that things will get worse if they say anything. Sometimes the offender is the breadwinner in the family and they need that to live on. They fear being homeless or not being able to pay the bills. They are bound by the fear of man, as we read in Proverbs 29:25: "The fear of man brings a snare," and they haven't yet learned the principle of trusting the Lord, as is stated in the rest of this verse: "but whoever trusts in the Lord shall be safe." Then there are enablers who simply don't care and by virtue of their silence the offender continues to harm others. The principle found in this well-known saying "All that is necessary for the triumph of evil is that good men do nothing." (Edmund Burke)

Jesus said in Matthew 24:12 "that the love of many will grow cold." Enablers have many reasons why they protect offenders, but it has nothing to do with love.

5
The Consequences

The consequences of abuse begin with the victim and spread out from there like shock waves from an earthquake carrying havoc and destruction as they go. The offender seems little concerned with the pain they cause. The statistics can count the individuals who are abused but they cannot begin to give a total picture of the disaster. The husband or wife, who marries someone who has been abused, will enter into their world and truly get a close-up look at the damage the offender has caused.

I grew up in the country and am used to being in the outdoors. I love to hike, and used to spend a lot of time camping and fishing as a teenager. There have been two times in my life when I have been lost in the woods. At first I thought everything was going fine and I was enjoying myself and God's creation. Then there came a point, when I realized something wasn't right. I still remember the feeling, when I realized I was not going in the direction that I thought I was. I was disoriented and almost dizzy, I don't remember being afraid but I was frustrated and not sure which direction to go. A child, who has been abused, often loses their moral compass. What they know inside to be wrong their offender tells them is okay. This is especially true when the offender is supposed to be a spiritual role model --everything in the victim's life is turned upside down. A family member or someone they trusted may have started showing them a lot of attention. It may have even seemed nice at first, but then this adult begins touching them and saying things that are confusing and that don't make any sense.

Sometimes offenders groom their victims by flattering them, buying them things, or doing something special for them. When an adult spends a lot of time with a child, who is not theirs, especially when they try to isolate the child so that they have time alone with them, that should be a warning sign for mom or dad to intervene. It is not a guarantee that there is evil intent, but we must be vigilant in protecting our children.

When a child is abused, they become confused and disoriented about life, and have trouble determining what is right and wrong, and who they can trust. For Faith, when her dad began raping and molesting her, she felt like she had nowhere to turn. Her mom was the breadwinner in the family, and therefore not home in the daytime. Her dad was also her pastor so she couldn't go to the church to share information about the abuse. Her home life was a nightmare, with her father screaming and yelling. He would physically abuse her brothers and emotionally abuse her mother. The constant fights and threats of suicide were used by her father to beat the family into submission and allow him to practice his evil.

The consequences to the victim come in several forms: emotional, physical, and psychological. The damage involves, literally, every emotion. Think of all your emotions, and name them one by one, and consider how being sexually or physically abused would affect them. Love is a beautiful and positive emotion that brings warmth, security, happiness and a sense of well-being. When a child is sexually assaulted by a parent or someone in authority over them, it shatters the definition of love and they no longer know the true meaning or feeling of love. They will carry this into their adult life, where they may find it very difficult to love or even to accept love, in its true form.

Trust is shattered when the one who was supposed to be caring for you, has violated you instead. One woman who came to us shared that she had gone to a pastor, as a young lady, for help and counseling, but he molested her each time she would come for help. Her trust was broken and she bears the scars to this day. Even if the parent is not the offender, if they fail to help to protect the child, the child will feel that they can trust no one. In many cases, children fear that if they go to the authorities, the police or their teachers at school that they will not be protected from their offender or they may fear that their offender will face harsh reprisals. Their entire sense of security is now gone—it has been completely shattered.

I remember when I graduated from high school and it was time to get a job and think about college, it was a rude awakening. It was not until then that I realized the security that I had as a child. Mom and dad took care of everything, they worked, they paid the bills, they fed us and clothed us, and if there were problems in life, they took care of them. Every child should be able to grow up with love and security, but when a child goes through abuse, they feel betrayed and vulnerable, and that insecurity usually follows them into adulthood.

I was introduced to a young man at a Bible study I was attending and when I told him about our ministry which deals with sexual abuse, he immediately started talking about his marriage. His wife was a victim of sexual abuse and that abuse was having a huge impact on the intimacy in their marriage. Meaningful intimacy is vital for a healthy marriage. There is a reason that the Holy Spirit inspired Paul to write to the believers at Corinth with this careful guidance for married couples. Let's look at 1 Corinthians 7:3-5: "let the husband render to his wife the affection due her, and likewise also the wife to her husband. The wife does not have authority over her own body, but the husband does. And likewise the husband does not have authority over his own body, but the wife does. Do not deprive one another except with consent for a time that you may give yourselves to fasting and prayer, and come together again so that Satan does not tempt you because of your lack of self-control." The horrors of abuse and its memories kill intimacy--which in turn can destroy a marriage. In some cases the spouse is aware of the abuse and at least knows the reason for some of their struggles. In many cases, the one who was abused never shares with their spouse what has happened to them. So the spouse has no idea why they are struggling, not only in their sex life, but with intimacy in general. This causes doubt, frustration, anger, mistrust, and resentment--as well as pain which leads to a sense of being unfulfilled. In the passage of I Corinthians 7, God stresses the importance of a healthy sexual relationship between the husband and the wife. So much so, that the only time when there should not be physical fulfillment and pleasure, is when they are so burdened over something, that they both decide to fast and pray. I can only imagine that to someone who has gone through abuse that this passage may bring about a negative response, because their offender forced themselves on them and on their body. That was evil and it was wrong and is something that God hates.

When marriage is what it should be, with the husband loving his wife and the wife respecting her husband and neither of them ever having been abused, this passage is much easier to understand and follow. Unfortunately, to the one who has been abused, the thought of someone else having authority over their body can be terrifying. Both the one abused, and their spouse, need to work on their understanding of God's Word, as well as understanding the devastation of sexual abuse and how it will impact their marriage.

The offender has stolen something very precious that God never intended them to have. Physical intimacy is something beautiful that God made to be fully enjoyed by the husband and wife. Often for the victims, sex and sexual activity is something they have come to despise and dread. Many of the chronic problems in marriage such as: sexual brokenness, pornography, unfaithfulness, lack of trust, poor communication, anger, fighting, etc., are the aftermath of childhood sexual abuse. Many unhealthy marriages are a result of an offender's sin. This may be one of the reasons that the concept of mutual submission is so difficult for many to accept. For example when a girl has been sexually assaulted by a man who had authority over her, the thought of submitting herself to her husband has to be unsettling.

There are several issues that need to be discussed when it comes to what mutual submission in the marriage relationship could mean. The word, submit, does mean to be under obedience. In a godly marriage, mutual submission should work because the husband loves his wife and cherishes her and always seeks to put her first over his own desires. The wife also loves and respects her husband. Most of the time we quote Ephesians 5:22 " wives submit yourselves to your own husbands, as to the

Lord." The wife is under her husband's leadership but the text goes on to say that the husband is to love his wife as Christ loves the church. Submission only does what God intends, when there is a loving leader.

Far too often the wife has been told to stay in a relationship even if it is abusive. There's no place in God's Word where He tells the wife to submit to beatings, emotional harm, or to subject her children to sexual or physical abuse. Too many times, we have heard stories from women who were told by their pastor or church leaders to stay in these harmful situations. Physical, emotional or sexual abuse toward the wife breaks the marriage covenant. Some of the behaviors of these misguided partners in marriage is criminal and needs to be reported to the police. The Biblical answer is that the abusive person should be arrested. It is important for society and for the church to support the victim in order to deliver the oppressed out of the hand of their abuser.

What so often has been overlooked is that in Ephesians 5:21, Paul exhorts every Christian to submit to one another. This goes far beyond the married couple. Mutual submission is a marvelous principle that should be the motivation of everyone in a loving Christian community. When is the last time that you have heard a preacher say, that husbands are to be submissive? It is the same Greek word as Paul uses in reference to the wife being submissive. Another overlooked fact is what God says in I Corinthians 7:4 that the husband does not have power over his own body but the wife does. Yes God has given the leadership role in marriage to the husband, in the same sense that there are leaders in any organizational structure, but only God is sovereign and no place in the Bible does God say that women or children must live in abuse. The church must stop excusing men who are abusive and stop tolerating their sinful behavior. Church leaders must stop misrepresenting God's Word by telling wives to stay with abusive husbands and/or leave their children in dangerous situations.

There are consequences to the victim's children. Faith shares in her testimony that the many years of rape and abuse by her father caused her to die emotionally. When dad molested Faith's niece and Faith had to come forward with her story, we had to tell our children what had happened to Faith when she was growing up. When Faith told our second oldest son, he said "That explains a lot." We were both caught off guard by what he said. Faith was always a kind and loving wife and mother, but she was emotionally wounded. Our children missed out on a lot because Faith did not express joy or excitement very well--she seldom would cry or speak out in public. The ripple effect of this one man's sin seems to have kept on going throughout the family.

6
The Wall

There seems to be an impenetrable wall of Secrecy that surrounds the church. This wall serves as a barrier to keep people from dealing with this Sin. There are many Christian ministries that are trying to address this issue within the church, but many pastors and church leaders want to keep these groups out of their church. If you Google search 'sexual abuse' you will find a long list of organizations and individuals who are dealing with this issue. While they are not all Biblically based, many of them are, and these could be a great help to the church in dealing with abuse. Some churches and organizations will allow discussion on sexual abuse but only if the dialogue refers to the victims and what they must do to forgive and move on with their lives. In other words, only part of the sexual abuse issue is acceptable to talk about in many Christian circles. By that I mean the 'positive' side of the story, like when a victim has a 'success' story to tell. When a survivor has overcome their abuse and forgiven their abuser and moved on with their life, the positive side of that story is acceptable for most church leaders, but to talk about the darkness of the sin and the truth about offenders and the need to hold them accountable for their sin, is not acceptable to talk about.

It looks like a few celebrities are invited to share their testimonies and talk about this tragedy in their lives because that part of the abuse story is acceptable and doesn't upset the apple cart or rock the boat. Many of our church leaders want to keep the 'status quo' when it comes to the issue of sexual abuse and any attempt to change that is rejected. The 'status quo' could be defined here as "don't touch it with a 10 foot pole". But very few are truly dealing with the sin and teaching Biblical guidelines for dealing with the offender and holding them accountable for their crimes. But too few people ever get through this "wall" and have access to churches and Christian ministries. And those that do gain access stay within the boundaries of what the leaders deem to be acceptable.

Early in our ministry, Faith sent out letters to 51 different Christian Colleges. The letters included her testimony and information on our ministry along with the statistics on sexual assault and its impact on the church. We encouraged them to deal with this growing and devastating sin and offered our services, if that would be helpful for them. We shared that the colleges were a great place to integrate our kind of ministry, since they were training the next generation of pastors, missionaries, and Christian workers. In total, we received three responses back from the 51 letters. One was polite but stated that they didn't need our help. The second was from the administrator of the "Christian" college who said, "He did not want to deal with this issue because he was afraid people would focus on it." The third letter was similar to the second.

In the next chapter, I want to look at why this wall exists and why it must come down. Over the years we have corresponded with many pastors, missionaries, Christian radio stations, and Christian cable channels in an effort to bring attention to this sin. We have found that the reluctance to even talk about sexual abuse is very strong. Many churches respond to our attempts at establishing a dialogue by saying that they do background checks on those that work in their children's ministries, as though that is somehow going to stop this sin. That seems to be their rationale that people in places of leadership and influence don't need to talk about sexual assault in an intentionally public way.

Fears that Build the Wall

Loss of Membership.

I was watching a movie about a person who was passing through a small western town. There was something very strange about the people there. The town's folk didn't like newcomers around and were very reluctant to carry on a conversation about their town. This newcomer soon realized there was some dark secret about the town's past that kept the people enslaved in secrecy. This story demonstrates something that resonates with people when they look at the state of affairs in many churches today.

There seems to be a tendency in many places to shy away from difficult issues, such as sexual assault, domestic violence, drug addiction, pornography and so on. We, who are part of the local church, often put on a nice face and appear to be a godly group of believers, but when someone begins to talk about these issues, it quickly makes the listeners very uncomfortable, especially when someone starts asking questions about the raping and molesting of children. Often the atmosphere in a Christian setting will change as many pastors and leaders do not want to talk about these issues. They would prefer to affirm that: "This just doesn't happen around here" or "We don't have any problems around here like that. These things are everyone else's problem, but not ours."

For example, when a victim comes forward with an accusation about sexual assault in the church, they are so often told to: be quiet and forgive the offender. This is so harmful to a victim. Frequently they are shunned, told to find another church, or even that they are the ones who have sinned. Church leadership so often fears that a scandal will hurt attendance. And while that may be a valid concern the first priority needs to be the safety and well-being of the victim. Since churches are constantly competing and searching for people to attend their churches then anything that might be a threat to church growth must be avoided. Churches can't take the chance that they might lose members.

When Faith's dad molested her niece, there was a need to bring this out in the open, not only to our family, but also to our congregation because he was a member of the church. This action, of making the church community aware about this man's damaging sexual transgressions, caused some people to make a decision to leave the church.

Since Faith's father failed to show any signs of repentance, it was necessary to practice church discipline.

In so many church communities, instead of dealing with the sin and the offender, who causes so much hurt to many individuals, the choice is to look the other way, for the "collective good". One victim told us about rampant sexual abuse by a faculty member of a Christian school. When some of the families learned of these sexual assaults, they went to the church leadership and the pastor warned these congregants to be quiet or there would be consequences. To the victim's knowledge these cases of sexual assault were never reported to the authorities and unfortunately, this faculty member is still employed there to this day.

A serious question arises: How many children are we going to sacrifice on the altar of fear before we wake up and be the people that God has called us to be? When the children of Israel were at the worst time morally in their history and were ripe for judgment, God said in Jeremiah 7:30, 31 "They have set their abominations in the house, which is called by My name, to pollute it. To burn their sons and daughters in the fire, which I did not command, nor did it come into my heart." Consider the words spoken to them by the prophet, Jeremiah and ask yourself the question "Is the behavior of many churches today, any different than God's people in the days of Jeremiah?" Every time a church looks the other way or refuses to protect the children that God has sent to them, they are little different than those who sacrificed their children in the fire so long ago. This passage demands our attention. Our prayer is that Christians recognize how damaging sexual abuse is and how it harms individuals and families. Yet, a further harm to those wounded, is when a church does nothing about it. There is a danger when the local church chooses to avoid its responsibility in dealing with this huge issue and victims are left without remedy.

Loss of Finances.

Many church leaders are afraid of how this will impact the finances of the church or organization. It probably will impact the finances, but does that justify not supporting victims and allowing offenders to go unchecked and in effect building a wall of protection around the sin? The real 'bottom line' is: What kind of dollar value does a church put on its children? How much money is it worth to look the other way? I am amazed that so many Christian organizations are willing to ignore this issue.

I received an email not long ago from a ministry that I have great respect for. They said that their ministry has a 'well defined program' but they don't feel that they are called to deal with this issue! Too many Christian groups do not feel that they need to be bothered with raising awareness and dealing with the issue of sexual abuse. Many seem to be quick to excuse themselves from any responsibility regarding abuse.

Christian organizations, pastors, missionaries, and countless Christian leaders have a responsibility to help the weak and those who have no voice. This is an opportunity for Christians to take a stand, to support, and be a positive influence for justice. It is unfortunate when Christian leaders, who could be a cause for righteousness and could influence their congregations to take up the cause of the oppressed, choose rather to absolve themselves of any responsibility to help the abused, because they are too busy doing other things for the Lord. I wonder what God would say about that? It is time for caring Christians and conscientious churches to get involved in being pro-active in these needy areas.

I telephoned a lady that I had known as a teenager, her husband had been serving in a church with a large Christian College for many years. As we talked, I shared information about the ministry that God had called us to. As I began to tell her about Faith's experience of sexual abuse and how God was leading us to help educate the church about biblical guidelines for dealing with abuse. She soon cut me off and stated that "if it really were God's will, the doors would open immediately." She went on to tell about how quickly the doors had opened for them. Her implication was that if churches are not willing to be open to dealing with this issue, then it should be obvious that it must not be God's will for us to attempt to deal with it. This seems to be a common attitude because most people are uncomfortable talking about sexual abuse issues, which are especially rooted in the church. They simply want to avoid the subject. Although this may be a difficult subject to tackle at any time, there is still a need for skilled people in the church to take this on. It is imperative to raise awareness about this issue as well as to find ways for those who see this need, to be intentional about it. The time of avoiding and looking the other way has come to an end. Since the media has brought many of these issues forward, society and the local church is much more willing to be involved in exposing sexual perpetrators.

So what are the church leaders, who refuse to deal with this issue, really saying? That maybe it is ok for people to rape and molest children after all? While no one would ever say that, by their inaction, that is exactly the perception that they are conveying. What is God going to have to do to bring the church to its knees? With many church budgets faltering monthly and many Christian colleges hoping for the large endowments that will finally be able to get them over the hump, the last thing they want is a scandal, but shouldn't there be something said about God's will and His blessing. God can do more in 5 minutes than we have been able to do in the last 50 years of combined effort. If God withdraws His blessing, all the money in the world can't build a church. Remember the verse that says "except the Lord builds the house, they labor in vain to build it." So, how can

God fully bless a local church when it may have knowingly or unknowingly built a wall of protection around one of the most heinous of all sins? And if you think that is an overstatement, then why did Jesus give such a graphic warning, in Luke 17:2, to those who abuse children? The church can labor all it wants, they can preach from the pulpit, send missionaries to foreign fields, give their money to help the poor, and they can pray for God's blessing, but a biblical case can be made that it is all in vain if we don't deal with this sin. For a church to effectively deal with the issue of sexual abuse, will take time and effort, but in the end may restore God's blessing.

The Pandora's Box.

There is the fear that if the leaders in the local church begin to deal with this sin, it will open a Pandora's Box that may lead to catastrophe for their ministry. An attorney who we talked to about this issue shared that he was on the boards of a number of large organizations, and it was his custom to routinely remind them that: "whenever a report of abuse came up, they needed to deal with it fully." In his experience, he sadly reported that in most cases they would give in to the mistaken belief that if they tried to hide or suppress the reports, that there would be less damage to the organization. He confirmed that, consistently, it was always the opposite. When people choose to deny and try to cover up a revealed sexual assault incident, (which is a crime), then they have to face the consequences of that poor choice and are forced to deal with the ensuing scandal. The fear of the damage that they might face was now part of their church leadership experience. They saw, firsthand, how it did damage to the reputation of their organization. A cover up only leads to shame, mistrust, more litigation, and very often, criminal charges.

The Penn State scandal that came to light in the fall of 2011 is a good example of this. Sandusky, who was the assistant coach for the college's famed football program, was accused of raping young boys, who he met through an organization that he founded. This group, called "Second Mile", was started to help troubled teens. One of the rapes was allegedly witnessed and reported to the head coach, who in turn reported it to a higher authority at the college, but apparently nothing was reported to the law. Consequently, there were more victims and in the end more damage.

The head couch was fired along with others who failed to act, the shame of what happened and the cover up that took place will last for many years. Shortly after the news broke about the scandal at Penn State, there was a story in the Canadian papers that the oldest Bible College in Canada had been covering up abuse for years. Many stories had surfaced about rapes, sexual assaults, and beatings that had been allowed. To date there are claims that as many as over ninety survivors have surfaced, many of whom are afraid to speak out publically, but those that have are awaiting justice. The public image of these organizations had taken many years to build, and once the reports began coming out, it only took a few days to tarnish their reputation. Many Christian organizations are afraid that being honest and searching for the truth when reports of abuse surface, will open their Pandora's Box.

Lawsuits

The leaders of both large and small churches fear the lawsuits that could come when someone has been abused by a church leader or a staff member. There are, of course, times when the victim or the victim's family will sue no matter what.

But we have heard of many stories, where the only thing the victim wanted was for the church to apologize; to say that they were sorry for what the victim had gone through. Christians who have been sexually assaulted by clergy would like to have the church community respond to them biblically, with love and encouragement for those who have been abused and to turn the offender over to the law and to hold the perpetrators accountable before the church. But when the church responds in an inappropriate way, the victims feel that they have no recourse but to sue through the courts in order to receive justice.

There are a couple of attorneys, from Texas, who go into churches and teach steps to help prevent child abuse, thereby limiting the church's exposure to lawsuits. They are very committed to the cause of protecting children and many churches will have them come in and teach, as long as it helps them prevent a law suit. The picture that this behavior seems to paint is that many church cultures seem more concerned about money issues than they are about whether or not children are being raped and molested by their church ministers or volunteers.

Self-Incrimination.

Then there is the fear of self-incrimination. If a church leader does deal with this sin, they may wind up exposing their own immorality and the immorality of their "inner circle." Some would call this "cronyism". Webster's dictionary states that cronyism is a term that refers to partiality to cronies or longstanding friends. The only way that sexual abuse, within an organization, can go on for so long without being exposed, is if there is some kind of cooperative effort by those in the "inner circle" to cover it up. It is one buddy, watching out for another. I am convinced, by the reactions that we have received from many of the Christian organizations that we have contacted, that this is a major problem in getting the church to deal with abuse.

There have recently been a number of court trials that have made the national news, where judges have sentenced convicted sex offenders to shockingly light sentences or no jail time at all! The first thing to cross my mind is that this is a form of cronyism, possibly even from one offender to another. The judge may not have known the individual personally, but when a child has been so horribly abused and the offender is found guilty yet the judge slaps him on the wrist, we must ask ourselves why? And many of the stories we have heard, where a prominent figure in the church has been accused of sexual assault and the leadership of the church tries to cover it up, we have to wonder if it is the same cronyism that motivates them to keep it quiet.

Hurt the name of Christ

Then there is the fear that when reports of abuse become public knowledge that this information will hurt the efforts of the church or ministries, who are trying to lead people to Christ. This is actually a very common concern that well-meaning Christians will bring up during our discussions. My response to that is: Have we absolutely lost our minds! It is the sin that hurts the work of Christ and brings shame to the church --not exposing it, not telling the truth about it and not dealing with it. Why would God tell people to "expose" the works of darkness, if doing so would hurt His work? Faith and I have also heard this "concern" in many of the places where we have presented our program during conferences and when we have spoken in churches. It would be appropriate to ask: Will dealing with abuse and holding offenders accountable for their sin hurt the name of Christ?

Ephesians 5:11 - 13 reminds Christians to: "Have no fellowship with the unfruitful works of darkness, but rather expose them. For it is shameful even to speak of those things which are done by them in secret. But all things that are exposed are made manifest by the light, for whatever makes manifest is light." We are commanded by God to expose evil. Again, it is the sin that hurts the name of Christ, not exposing it. If there is ever a biblical mandate for dealing with this sin, it is right here in these verses. It is safe to conclude that: if a church fails to expose the truth about abuse and biblically deal with it, then there is little or no light in that church. There are misbeliefs, and fears which get in the way of making right decisions when it comes to this issue. Christians need to be aware of them, in order to be informed, to be vigilant, and to take appropriate action when needed. God's will is that these works of darkness need to be exposed. And that it is the light that exposes the evil.

Pain and Suffering

Another reason why many Christians fear dealing with this sin is because once it is known, it will cause pain and suffering for so many people. I believe the majority of the people who look the other way, do so because they cannot bear the thought of how much pain this is going to cause. The plain fact is: once the sin of sexual assault has been committed, there is no painless answer. There is no easy way out or quick fix. In many cases, the people close to the victim often refuse to let the victim testify because of what they will go through during the trial. But when this happens, there is no justice or resolution for the child and the healing process is not truly allowed to begin.

Choosing what seems to be the easier way or the least painful way out of a very bad situation, only adds to the distress.

When adults fail to consider the long-term damage that will be done to the child, the child is re-victimized. When, for whatever reason, the story of what has happened is suppressed, it only reinforces what the offender has already told the victim... no one loves them, they are dirty, it is their fault, no one will believe them, etc. The Bible exhorts those who love Christ: to support the weak. Once a child has been sexually assaulted, it is too late to stop the initial damage, but God has called the church to help the hurting individual to walk through the painful process of healing as well as the process of holding the offender accountable.

Denial

Fear and selfishness builds the wall that protects the sin and the offenders, but denial also plays a role in this wall. It is the bury-your-head-in-the-sand syndrome. I remember when Faith and I were talking to a friend of ours about our ministry and telling them for the first time about Faith's story. We were still talking, when this lady chimed in that "We don't have this problem at our church." I thought back many years, to when I knew a lot of the people from her church. I thought about the mother who was afraid that her husband was molesting their five year old daughter. I thought about the man who used to attend the church, who always told the pastor to preach a hell fire and brimstone message--but I found out later that he had raped every one of his daughters. I thought about the man who used to put up signs in his yard that had verses on them, which he changed throughout the year--he had raped his daughters. I thought about the young woman who was getting married and when someone mentioned about her dad, who was a heavy drinker, walking her down the aisle, she said "no way, I have more respect for a dog than I have for him." He also had sexually abused his daughters. I thought about the grandparents who were concerned that their son-in-law was abusing their grandchildren. I thought about another young lady who was getting married and had been molested by an older girl. Those were just the stories I know of and this doesn't include the missionaries or the mission board which the church supported, that was later found out to be fraught with abuse--but this "wasn't happening at my church" Oh yes it was, but she just didn't know it. This is one reason that it is so important for churches to be more open when they are dealing with these issues. A lack of knowledge only keeps people in the dark and gives offenders more opportunities to harm others. The congregation should be well informed of what has happened and what is being done to deal with it. Bill Anderson's book *When Child Abuse Comes to Church* is a good model for churches to use when dealing with abuse. Some people have their heads buried so far in the sand that only their toes are sticking out. Denial allows church folks to stay in ignorance and be comfortable there. At first it may seem strange that denial can help build a wall, but if we deny a sin's existence, then the very denial becomes an obstacle that must be overcome before we can move on to confession, repentance, and healing. How many times have we heard that the first thing an alcoholic has to do, before they can be "cured," is to admit that they have a problem?

There is an account in 2 Kings 5 that tells a story about Naaman the leper. Naaman had experienced healing from his leprosy, under the ministry of the prophet, Elisha. Though Elisha had refused the gifts of goods and money that Naaman had offered him, his servant, Gehazi, wanted these gifts. When Elisha had gone inside and Naaman was leaving to begin his journey home,

Gehazi followed and caught up with him and lied about some last minute guests coming to visit and that Elisha had changed his mind and would accept some of the gifts.

The reason I mention this story is that when Gehazi comes back and hides these gifts, Elisha confronts him and asks where he went. Gehazi chooses to deny what he had done. His <u>denial cost him dearly</u>, it cost him a chance to confess, it cost him a chance to repent, it cost him a chance for forgiveness and mercy. The leprosy of Naaman came into his body and brought him the disease for the rest of his life. This disease was even passed down through his family for generations. When church leadership chooses to deny that sexual abuse is occurring, they are, in effect, helping it to continue and they bring on themselves and their churches the "leprosy" of abuse and all the suffering that goes with it. These consequences may go on for generations.

Pride

Pride is another part of the wall that surrounds this sin. In 1 Corinthians 5 ,Paul says, "it is actually reported that there is sexual immorality among you, and such sexual immorality as is not even named among the gentiles, that a man has his father's wife! And you are puffed up, and have not rather mourned, that he who has done this deed might be taken away from among you." Pride is what allows us to see the sin in other churches or in other denominations, but not in our own. Pride blinds Christians from the truth. In this passage we have a local church in the city of Corinth, a lot like our churches today in that they wrestled with issues of sin and immorality. This man, who was a part of the church, was not only committing sexual sin, but it was so bad that even the pagans were astonished with this brazen lifestyle. It could be that this person brought his lifestyle with him when he came to Christ and maybe continued to live that way. Even the pagans knew that living sexually with one's father's wife was out of their normal cultural boundaries and that was a very immoral culture. Paul doesn't directly address this man but rather his main focus is with the church and how they did not deal with it. This man's sinful life style was known to the people of the church and yet they had done nothing to take any reasonable action.

It is 'why' they had done nothing that interests me here. The reason they had done nothing was because of their arrogance. Paul says that they were puffed up and had not rather mourned. The condition of many churches today is one of pride and stubbornness, and as long as that continues the wall will remain standing. Christians are unable to mourn when they are arrogant.

There is a great need for the church to mourn for the children who have lost the innocence that God intended them to have in their childhood. They have lost their joy and sense of self-worth and, in many cases, their reason for living. I fear that too many in the Christian community are puffed up, like the Corinthian church and are unprepared to respond to the cries of those who have been sexually assaulted.

Not long ago, Faith was on the telephone talking with someone whose daughter had been molested by a person at her church. This lady had done a lot of research on the ministries that are available to help churches deal with sexual abuse. When she asked her pastor about getting one of these ministries to come to their church, he said he wouldn't have them come because "it is too complex of a situation and that no one else outside of their church would understand." This pastor's pride was keeping him from helping his church deal with the abuse that had harmed their children. This pastor's reaction is played out time and time again in churches throughout our country. Pride may indeed be the oldest sin of all, as it was Satan's pride that caused him to rebel against God. And it is the pride of our church leaders that is keeping many of them from taking down this wall of silence and secrecy, which would allow those trained and skilled in this issue to more effectively deal with it .

In 2 Samuel 24, we read the account of David, who was the king of Israel, telling Joab, the captain of his army, to count the people of Israel, in other words, do a census. David said, "I want to know how many people we have in our country." The problem here was that God had commanded the leaders of the children of Israel not to number them because He did not want their leaders to put their trust in how many people were in the nation. He wanted Israel to always trust and rely on Him only. When King David asked Joab to number the people, he knew that it was wrong, but being motivated by his pride, as a king, he wanted to know. Even though Joab pleaded with David not to do this, the king stubbornly refused his counsel. David's pride prompted him to sin and that caused God to send a plague throughout Israel as judgment. This plague killed tens of thousands of people. Soon after the plague, David realized his sin and repented, but much damage was already done. Many local church leaders are allowing their pride to prevent a remedy for this pervasive practice of ignoring the incidences of sexual abuse in the church. It is the sin of the offenders that is doing the initial damage, but it is the pride of many of our church leaders that is keeping this sin alive and well. It is pride that is causing leaders to reject biblical and common sense solutions that would hold offenders accountable. That is exactly what was happening in the Corinthian church. If Paul were here today, he would give a scathing report on many churches that resist taking action when they could be pro-active about this type of situation in their churches.

Steps to Tearing Down the Wall

So what is the process that we need to undertake in bringing down this wall, just as there are a number of factors that went into building up the wall, there are a number steps that we must go through to help bring down this wall. Let's look at six steps that will help tear down this wall.

Step number one, stop the arrogance and pride. Step number two, stop the denial. Step number three, stop the excuses. Step number four, stop minimizing the sin. Step number five, stop breaking the law. And step number six, stop hurting the victims.

Stop the Pride

Let's start first of all with the pride issue. In the I Corinthians passage, the answer to their being 'puffed up' is given in the same sentence. Paul says "You have not rather mourned". The antidote to pride is humility and mourning. Pastors and Christians should be on their knees before God with tears in their eyes and a broken heart, pleading with God for forgiveness and for the wisdom to help minister to those who are hurting from abuse. And we should be asking God to help us have the strength to hold offenders accountable. Because their pride had allowed this evil to be practiced and the offender was unchecked and un-confronted, the paganism practiced all around them paled in comparison. The church today is so quick to condemn the evils of our society, but we are willfully blind to what is in our own midst. It's like the elephant in the room that everybody else can see, but we pretend does not exist. The world sees our hypocrisy and rather than being a beacon of light that is drawing the world to Christ, we are all too often turning people away. One church we were at in Michigan, where the pastor had been arrested for abusing a child, told us that a number of parents pulled their children out of church and told their children "that's why we don't go to church." I wonder how many people in the world, who are not attending church, stay away because of the ungodliness they see from the people who attend. It is true that the gospel of Christ is an offense to the world, because God says there's only one way to get to heaven and that way is through Jesus Christ and what he did for us on the cross, and that will offend many, but we're not to be an offense ourselves, because of our hypocrisy. The day needs to come, when the whole body of Christ needs to see this sin for what it is and be truly sickened by it and fall on their knees in mourning, repent and confess to God, for not dealing with this, generations ago. Lest you are tempted to say that you don't have a need to mourn and confess because you have not been a part of this sin, don't forget that Daniel, when he realized that the seventy years of captivity were nearly over, he prayed and confessed the sin of Israel and included himself, as he asked God for forgiveness.

Stop the Denial

Not only do we have to deal with the issue of pride, but the next thing we have to deal with is denial. This wall will never come down unless we stop the denial. When we talk about denial we are talking about denying the truth, about the sin of sexual abuse. It is difficult for us to grasp and accept the fact that the evil of child sexual abuse exists in our midst. It is even more difficult to accept the prospect that it is prevalent today. Yet that is exactly what the statistics are showing us, consider the following reports:

It is estimated that one in three girls and one in six boys will experience some form of sexual abuse before they are18 years old. We get that statistic from the U.S. Department of health and human services, and that was from a 1993 study. The typical child sex offender molests an average of 117 children, most of whom did not report the offense. This data is from the national institute of mental health and the 1988 study.

Research indicates that most child sexual abuse takes place in the home, but news reports constantly remind us that such abuse can also be found in churches, and that even many pastors and church leaders have been found guilty of the offense.

This is especially evil because the violation is taking place at the hands of those who are entrusted with a responsibility to lead and protect the sheep. It is particularly abominable when the protector becomes the predator. If fulfills the warning of Jude 1:4 where God says "certain men who were designated for this judgment long ago, have crept in unawares. They are godless men who turn the grace of our God into a license to sin." In verse 4 God warns of evil men coming into the church and committing sexual sin and then using the beautiful gift of God's grace as an excuse or license to commit one sexual sin after another.

Our first response, when faced with evidence that members of our church family or leadership are guilty of these horrible offenses, often is disbelief and denial. We do not want to believe that such a thing can happen in our midst, so we convince ourselves that it never really happened.

Tragically, when we deny the sin, it enables offenders to continue in their sin and further intimidates victims into not speaking up. They fear no one will believe them.

Consider the example of king Saul in 1 Samuel 15: 20 Where Saul said to Samuel, "but I have obeyed the voice of Lord, and done the mission which the Lord sent me, and brought back Agag king of Amalek and have utterly destroyed the Amalikites." God had commanded Saul to destroy all the inhabitants and animals, because their wickedness was great, but he chose to disobey. When Samuel confronted him with his disobedience, Saul's first response was denial. Despite the fact that Samuel could hear the bleating of the sheep and the lowing of the oxen, Saul continued to deny his disobedience.

The Lord expects His people to take appropriate action within the church when a member sins. Matthew 18 gives us the process that God wants us to follow in dealing with a member who sins.

While we might be tempted to say, that we are fully obeying the Lord, the cries of the victims of sexual abuse and the emotional heartache of those ravaged by this sin can be heard and seen all around us. When it comes to the issue of sexual abuse, too many pastors and church leaders are living in a state of denial, meanwhile, the sin continues to devastate the lives of those who attend their churches. So before the wall can be torn down, our pride must stop, our denial must stop and our excusing the sin must stop.

Stop Excusing The Sin

Once believers are confronted with the evidence of the sin and they're no longer able to deny it, they may be tempted to excuse the behavior. This is especially true when the offenders are prominent members, or even leaders in their churches. Their flawed reasoning holds that because the accused leaders have done so much good for the church, they should be excused. On the other hand, some Christians will overlook the behavior because of the potential consequences of dealing with this sin, such as; scandal, embarrassment, loss of revenue, civil lawsuits, criminal punishment etc. Some even claim that they are concerned that exposing the sin will bring reproach to the name of Christ. However it is that very sin and the failure to address it Biblically that brings shame to the name of Christ, not exposing it. Once again, let's look at the example of Saul. When Samuel indicated to Saul, that he knew Saul had brought back the animals that he was supposed to destroy, and Saul knew that he could no longer deny his sin, he chose to excuse the sin by saying, "the people took the sheep and the cattle." Saul excuses his disobedience by blaming others for what he had done. When they can no longer deny their actions, many offenders will excuse it by blaming the victims, other people, or their circumstances. In one recent case involving a pastor who had molested two children, the church people were blamed by the pastor's wife, because they were not praying hard enough for their pastor. Rather than hold her husband accountable it was easier for her to blame the church. When God confronted Adam with his sin; Adam blamed Eve and then he also blamed God for what he had done. He said "the woman whom you gave to be with me, she gave me and I ate." To excuse disobedience by blaming someone else is the oldest trick in the book. As hard as it is to believe, many offenders who claim to be Christians will blame God for their vile behavior. They say, "God made me do this", or "God gave me these desires". In each of these, the assumption is that because of various external circumstances, their actions are understandable and even excusable, but that reasoning will never stand up before God.

Excusing sexual abuse is neither loving nor forgiving. We must stop making excuses and start holding offenders accountable. I Corinthians 5: 11-12, teaches us that we are to judge those who are within. We hear frequently from well-meaning Christians, that we are not supposed to judge. And yet in these verses, God clearly says we are to judge those who are within the church. There is no end to the excuses that an offender will use to try to get away with their sin, but none of them are acceptable. It's time for the church to stop making excuses for the offenders.

Stop Minimizing The Sin

When an offender or church is confronted with the evidence of this sin, and when the sin can no longer be denied or excused, the abuser may attempt to minimize the sin and to convince others that it is not really as bad as it appears. Abusers will often say things like: we had an affair or we had an incestuous relationship, as if their evil desires were shared mutually between offender and victim. In their perverted minds, they somehow convince themselves that this is not rape or molestation, but rather a mutual relationship. Sexually abusing a child is evil and wrong, it is rape and should be called that. It is filthy and vile and the church should recognize it as such.

Each week we receive new reports from victims who were harmed by this sin. One such report was from a woman who, as a 15 year old pastor's daughter, was raped by a guest speaker who was staying in their home. He raped her and then spoke in their church as though nothing was wrong! He threatened that if she told anyone, terrible things would happen to her parents and that her father would have to leave the ministry, so she kept her secret. For years she thought she would go to hell, because of what her abuser had done to her. Another victim shared that as a young child she was raped and molested for many years by her father. In her heart wrenching story, she tried to describe her feelings of guilt and pain and how she thought others would think that she was dirty and this sense was so strong that she thought she gave off a foul odor. How sad for a child to be so harmed, that they bear the shame and guilt for what has been done to them It's not right that victims are burdened to carry the guilt and shame of the sin while the offenders go on with their lives as though nothing was wrong.

What these criminals are inflicting on their victims destroys them emotionally, and causes deep wounds that will last the rest of their lives. It not only devastates the lives of the victims, it does untold harm to the victim's relationships with their future spouses and children. There is nothing that could ever be presented that should allow an abuser or the church to minimize this sin.

Notice that Saul not only tried to deny and excuse his disobedience but he also tried to minimize the sinfulness of it, by reasoning with Samuel that the animals were saved to sacrifice to the Lord.

Proverbs 21:3 says, "to do what is right and just is more acceptable to the lord than sacrifice". There is no conscionable way that we can minimize this sin, yet because it is so troubling to believe that this is happening in the body of Christ, many are willing to deny, excuse, and minimize it, whatever it takes to ease their consciences.

Stop Breaking The Law

The Church body needs to realize and remember that this sin is also a criminal offense therefore we have a moral, logical, and legal obligation to treat it as such.

Consider what God says to the church in Romans 13:3-5, "For rulers are not a terror to good works, but to evil, do you want to be unafraid of the authority? Do what is good, and you will have praise of the same for he is God's minister to you, for good. But if you do evil, be afraid for he does not bear the sword in vain, for he is God's minister, an avenger, to execute wrath on him who practices evil. Therefore you must be subject not only because of wrath but also for conscience' sake."

When it comes to addressing this sin, churches too often are reluctant to turn offenders over to the law. They often have a misunderstanding of grace and justice, believing that it is unloving or unforgiving to hold an offender accountable before the law. For some reason, many conclude that somehow justice is wrong.

We read in Proverbs 18:5, "It is not good to be partial to the wicked or to deprive the innocent of justice." When we hide the sin we are being partial to the wicked. When we protect the offender we are being partial to the wicked. When we ask the victim not to tell anyone, we are depriving them of justice. When we fail to report offenders, we deprive the innocent of justice. Consider what Solomon says in Proverbs 17: 15, "Acquitting the guilty and condemning the innocent, the Lord detests them both". God despises the person who helps the offender escape the punishment of their crime. God despises the person who protects the offender from the consequences of their sin. God despises the person who condemns the innocent. When someone says that it was the victim's fault, God despises that person. That's not my word, that's what God says.

God's Word is clear. We are to love and forgive, but we must realize that love and forgiveness do not eliminate the consequences of our sin. The devastation that is heaped upon the victims of this sin is not erased by a simple apology, nor are the legal and personal debts of an offender satisfied with an apology.

We recognize this with other criminal activities such as murder, assault, or theft, but for some reason, many are willing to simply overlook abusive behavior. Some may think it is too harsh for offenders to face the consequences of their choices, because they may lose their reputation, social standing, family, or freedom. When the abuse is brought to light, innocent people are heavily impacted; the family members of the offender, as well as the victims, face shame and loss. It is true that the process will bring pain to the guilty as well as to the innocent, but we are not relieved from a legal obligation. We must hold offenders accountable before God and the law.

Stop Hurting The Victims

One of the things, that we have personally experienced, and have seen many others go through, is that when victims come forward, they do not find love and support from their church and family members. While there were a few families, at our church, who excused Faith's dad's actions, the majority of our church has been very supportive. It is because of their support that we have been able to start this ministry to speak out against the sexual abuse of children. The enablers left soon after we held dad accountable and broke off fellowship with him. Many will respond with disbelief or assert that the victim needs to forgive and forget. While it is true that we need to be able to forgive, much of the time when victims are told to forgive and forget, what is really being said is, that they need to be quiet. Because the church and the family do not want to be embarrassed, inconvenienced, or forced to deal with the situation that makes them uncomfortable, the easiest thing to do is to pressure the victim to be quiet. This causes unimaginable damage and pain to the victim. In the book "Invisible Girls", the author states that the most important factor in victim's healing is being able to tell their story. If that is true, then what the church has been doing for generations (teaching the "forgive and forget" policy), is only bringing more harm to the victims, because we are saying you can't tell your story, when that is exactly what they need to do. When we tell the victim of sexual abuse to be quiet or we encourage them to suppress their story, essentially what we are telling them is that they do not matter. And what they have gone through is not serious enough for us to deal with. We devalue them as a person and as a child of God. What we are doing is, in fact, reinforcing the abuse that they experienced at the hands of their offenders. Often, victims are told that if they are struggling with the emotional and spiritual wounds of their abuse, it is a sign that they are unforgiving. How ridiculous is that! We don't accuse someone who has suffered physical abuse of being unforgiving if their broken bones don't heal immediately. But we judge a person who has been ravaged spiritually and emotionally by how quickly or slowly they heal. Jesus says in Luke 17: 2 that "offenses will come, but woe to him through whom they come! It would be better for him if a millstone was hung around his neck, and he was thrown into the sea, than for him to cause one of these little ones to stumble." In light of what Christ says in this passage about offenders, we must remember that our role as the body of Christ in these situations is to both help and comfort the victims, and firmly confront offenders in a Biblical way. What is happening in most churches and Christian organizations today is that offenders are being protected and the children are being pushed aside for the sake of the institution. God's judgment will be swift and severe and it will start in His house.

Until we take these steps we cannot begin to tear down the wall that has been built up over the years to protect this sin.

7
The Church's Role in Dealing with Abuse

I believe that only when the church is able to come together as the body of Christ and have a meaningful discussion of all the different aspects of this issue, will we ever come up with all the answers we need, to truly deal with this sin. For now there are some obvious answers that need to be considered.

What needs to be done in order to fully deal with abuse. The church, family members, victims, enablers, and offenders, all must follow the God-given biblical guidelines for dealing with this issue. God has set before us a clear path in His Word that gives us principles and guidelines for dealing with virtually any situation. We will first consider what the church needs to do.

If we're ever going to effectively deal with abuse, the church must get it right. The church has for too long muddled its way through this issue and for the most part has dealt with this according to the wisdom of man and not God. In the book, *Children and Sexual Abuse* one victim said that "the pastor, several of the church leaders, and various members in the church knew my sisters and I were being molested by my father. But no one in the church said or did anything. I heard plenty of sermons and Bible lessons teaching, that girls should not have sex before marriage. But I'd never heard anybody preach a sermon or give a warning to fathers not to have sex with their daughters." How sad is that? This is the message that our young people are hearing in our churches. They may be hearing one thing but seeing another. Is it any wonder that our young people are fleeing the churches in droves?

    We have recently been working with a group of believers, who are attending a church where the pastor has molested a fourteen year old girl, who was attending the church youth group. He pled guilty to the charges and received three weeks in jail. When the church was meeting to address the issue of what the pastor had done, some of the seniors of the church thought they should give the pastor a second chance. What does that mean? A second chance to do what? A second chance to get it right? A second chance to minister? Or a second chance to rape and molest another child? At one of their meetings between the church and the pastor, he acknowledged that he had molested the girl, but then he went on to say that she was a 'troubled' girl. He blamed her for what had happened and said that she had seduced him. After criticizing his victim, he began criticizing her mother. It was a classic attempt by the offender to make everyone else look bad in an effort to make what he had done look less evil. When the church turned to their denomination leadership for help, they did send a state representative to come and talk with them about abuse. After going through some brief training and telling the church how to protect themselves from a lawsuit, they felt that they had sufficiently dealt with the situation. There was no attempt to help the victim, to pay for counseling, or to reach out to the parents. It was all about the institution, not the people hurt by the abuse. One couple in this church had the conviction to take a stand. The representatives did nothing to address the spiritual issues that surround abuse; to them the most important thing was to get the situation behind them as soon as possible.

So what is the answer? What is it that the church needs to do? There are several aspects that the church needs to address in sexual assault situations. First, there is the legal aspect of this sin. It is a violent crime and the church must make sure the proper authorities are notified. This is not an option, it is the law and God gives us the Biblical mandate to recognize and utilize this authority in Romans 13 that we will look at later. The primary action the church must take is to make sure the victim is safe and the best way to do that is to let the law do its job. The system is not perfect and it will make mistakes, but God has put government in place to punish those who do evil. Any attempt to circumvent the law will only allow the offender the opportunity to rape and molest more children.

When Faith and I were attending a workshop dealing with sexual abuse, we were going over a case study wherein a prominent deacon in the church had molested a young teenage boy, from the same church. As the attendees were discussing the situation and what action the pastor should take once he heard about the accusation. A couple of people in our group insisted that the pastor should first 'determine' whether or not the story was true or credible. This may seem reasonable to most Christians, but the fact is that it is not the pastor's job to determine credibility. That is for law enforcement to decide.

Pastors are not investigators nor do they have the skills or legal authority to conduct an investigation. All too often church leaders take on that role only to wind up further endangering the victim and allowing the offender a chance to hide evidence and threaten anyone who may have knowledge of the particular incident, especially the victim. In short, they wind up hindering the ones that God put in charge of enforcing the law and tip-off offenders that their actions are known--thereby helping them to get away with what they have done.

When we recently dealt with a man who had molested a young teenage girl, I had a deacon, who was in his nineties lecture me for reporting a "Christian" offender to the law for what he had done. He went on to say that the church should deal with its own problems and not get the law involved. He then told me that he had a friend years ago, who had molested a girl and that their church had "handled" the situation. When I asked what the church had done to 'handle' it, he told me that they had talked with the offender and that he had moved away and went on with his life…. and probably continued molesting his children. He actually thought that that was the right response--and so do a lot of other Christians today. Why is it that so many Christians are willfully ignorant about what the Bible says? The answer is that the church has a moral and biblical obligation to report offenders to law and let the law do what God put them there to do. It is the investigator's job to determine if an accusation is credible, not ours.

If a child tells us, that they are being abused, we must report that to the authorities. To do anything less is a rejection of God's plan for dealing with evil in society. Again, in Roman's 13:1-5 we read Paul's words: "let every soul be subject to the governing authorities. For there is no authority except from God, and the authorities that exist are appointed by God. Therefore whoever resists the authority resists the ordinance of God, and those who resist will bring judgment on themselves. For rulers are not a terror to good works, but to evil. Do you want to be unafraid of the authority? Do what is good and you'll have praise of the same. For he is God's minister to you for good. But if you do evil, be afraid; for he does not bear the sword in vain; for he is God's minister, an avenger to execute wrath on him who practices evil. Therefore you must be subject not only for wrath but for conscience' sake."

When a church considers not reporting this crime to the proper authorities, they are contemplating rebellion against both the law of the land and the word of God. The old myth that churches are to provide sanctuary for criminals, may have had a place in history, but is certainly not a New Testament principle or a modern day convenience. There have been times in history and there may be times in the future when a government asks its people to do things that are clearly against the Bible. In those cases Christians will be compelled to obey God and not that government, but protecting those who perpetrate evil on children is not one of them.

The law has the authority to arrest a sexual offender and to get him away from a child or to take the child out of the dangerous situation. I know there may be some who object to taking a child out of a home since they may be vulnerable to abuse by others. This may be something to consider. But for the child who is presently being sexually assaulted in the home there must be immediate action to get them to the safety of another home. That is all the more reason for the church to stop being a sanctuary for offenders and to start being known as a place of safety for those who have been sexually abused. We are told by

God, to help and support the weak and afflicted and to rebuke and break off fellowship with those who walk disorderly. So the first part of the solution would be for the church to file reports of abuse with the proper authorities, so that they can fulfill their God-given responsibilities. But that is only the first part of the solution, of what the church must do. They also have to deal with the abuse at the church level, as well as the family level.

When both the victim and the sexual offender attend the same church, the ramifications reach most, if not all, of the people. Everyone is hurting, angry, and embarrassed. There are many questions about what will happen and how it will impact them and their home church. When it comes to a transgressing believer, God's Word gives us some very specific instructions on how to deal with that person. Let us look at several Scripture passages and discuss what they mean.

In Matthew 18:15, we read: "Moreover, if your brother sins against you go and tell him his fault between you and him alone. If he hears you, you have gained a brother. But if he will not hear, take with you one or two more, that by the mouth of two or three witnesses every word may be established. And if he refuses to hear them, tell it to the church. But if he refuses even to hear the church, let him be to you like a heathen and the tax collector."

Once the church has reported the sexual assault, to the law, it is time for the local church to focus on its God-given responsibility, which is ministering to the needs of those who have been harmed and impacted by the abuse.

It is important that the attention of the church be given to the victim or victims and their families, first. In cases where the sexual offender is not one of the child's parents, the church needs to work with both parents to determine how they can best help. An experienced Christian counselor is needed. It is important that a male counselor should never be assigned to counsel a female victim. Some may disagree with this and even scoff at the idea, but the stories are many, where girls go for counseling and are sexually assaulted by the male counselors. I am appalled at the number of situations, that we place men over women and young girls, where they are vulnerable to abuse. These include: girls' sports teams, counseling, camping events, and youth outings, to name a few. We are creating unnecessary opportunities for temptation and sexual abuse. Christians say they believe the Word of God, but so often practice something very different. There is a reason for the guideline found in Titus2:3-5--that the older women should teach the younger ones about the complex issues of life and godliness.

Churches need to have a plan in place for dealing with any incidences of sexual assault long before it occurs. Every church should establish a resource list of reputable Christian counselors, who are able to give biblical and professional help to victims. Churches should be prepared to offer financial assistance for this counseling. One of our first conferences was at a church in Albany, New York. The pastor at the church had already put a plan in place to deal with sexual abuse. He had a number of women in the church that had gone through sexual abuse or were familiar with the issue. These were godly and knowledgeable Christian women who he could count on and who he would refer girls and women to, who had experienced the trauma of sexual assault.

When sexual abuse is made known, the victim and their family members need help immediately. That is why a plan should be in place before an incident of sexual abuse occurs.

These ladies would help guide all those who were wounded through the process of sharing their stories and getting counseling and any other help that they needed. What often happens is that somebody in a local church will see the need for this in their church. Yet, when they go to their church leadership to see if their church will adopt policies and procedures for dealing with abuse, the leadership often promptly rejects the person's concerns. But before a church can truly prepare itself to deal with the aftermath of sexual abuse, it needs to educate itself as to the extent of abuse and how it impacts others.

After making sure that there are Christian counselors available and that funds are in place to help, the church needs to make sure that they have qualified people available within the church, to follow up with the victims and their families. However many churches might not be large enough, or have the resources to afford the qualified help, but they should have a 'resource' list, for church leaders, of qualified help in their area. Church leaders should compile this list for their area and be familiar with it.

Leading or helping to lead a support group for people who have gone through abuse can be a big help in the healing process. There are a number of groups and materials available that deal with this issue. One resource that Faith has used to lead a support group is called: "Surviving the Secret". Some of the best leaders and facilitators are those who have survived abuse and have gone through support groups themselves. I recently heard about a single mom who went through domestic abuse. She took a 'Living Waters' course and after 30 weeks, she was a changed woman and started working with other people in a "Living Waters' group at a nearby church as a helper. She later led her future husband to the Lord and moved back to Holland where he had a home and now they are doing Living Waters' courses there!

The church must remember that healing from sexual assault will take a lifetime. Far too many Christians think that once they have had a couple of meetings and the victims have had a little counseling that that solves everything and the victim should be able to get on with their lives. This only serves to demonstrate the extreme lack of knowledge that surrounds this issue, even among the so-called experts. I was listening to a radio ministry not long ago and they had an "expert" talking about the difficulties for victims after they had been abused. The expert said that they had written about it in their book and that they had dedicated a <u>whole</u> chapter to that issue. Good grief, the ignorance of many of our church leaders is colossal! A whole chapter, as though that was going to adequately deal with the issue. There are hundreds of books that deal with abuse, but all the books in the world cannot make up for the destruction that has taken place in someone's life when they have been abused. Unfortunately the conventional wisdom, even among Christians, seems to say to the victims, "You should be over it by now". I'm always frustrated with the ignorance and callousness that is prevalent among many of our church leadership and the so-called Christian experts when it comes to abuse. For example: Do we tell someone who has been maimed for life, because of an accident, that they are bitter or unforgiving or that they are not trying hard enough, because their body is not healed? Yet it would appear that this is exactly what all too many church leaders and experts are telling those who have been emotionally, physically, and psychologically devastated by sexual abuse.

The church needs to move in a positive direction by becoming a safe haven and a nurturing environment for those who have been abused; a place where Christ's love can be extended to those who are hurting. In order for this to happen, most churches need to be re-educated about this issue. There is a need to help change the faulty mindset that has held the church in ignorance. Bill Anderson in his book, *When Child Abuse Comes to Church*, strongly suggests that: "education is the first line of defense in protecting our children." The status quo is unacceptable, the old church leadership, who have either sat by and allowed this to continue or even helped cover it up, must either change their way of thinking or be replaced by those who will obey the mandates in God's word to protect and help the weak and oppressed.

The church should speak out and be open about this issue. While I was attending a conference at a Bible College in New York, I was listening to a very well-known speaker. He shared how his father had to leave the ministry because of a moral failure. I could see that this had impacted him greatly and I sensed that there might be an opportune moment to talk with him about the issue of sexual abuse and how Christian leaders need to speak out about it from church pulpits. Again I was surprised by his response. He resisted the idea that pastors needed to talk about sexual abuse openly, saying that if pastors simply preached about righteousness and sin in general that this somehow was going to cover the issue. So in other words, pastors would not need to address the issue of sexual assault as long as they just spoke about the need to live right and obey God's Word. That may sound fairly reasonable, but the reality is that it is imperative for church leaders to speak openly about sexual abuse. It is the status quo that has gotten us where we are today. It is time for pastors and churches to wake up and to grasp what is happening. If church leaders continue down the same path of ignoring this issue and somehow pretending that speaking about it in general terms is going to help, then there is a great danger that church leaders and congregants will be deceived and this sin will continue to harm people.

The church speaks openly about most topics; controversial issues are put forth all the time. For example we talk about sex before marriage, we talk about homosexuality, we talk about the end times, and the like. If we can talk about these issues openly, why can't we talk about the issue of sexual abuse openly? This speaker's attitude reflects the thinking that too many in the church have had for generations. It is time for this to change. This flawed mindset continues to allow a lack of knowledge among Christians on how to adequately respond to abuse.

Faith and I would have handled the aftermath of her sexual abuse much differently, if we had been taught what to do. Shortly after we started our ministry, Faith and I were discussing the fact that even though we both grew up in church, went to Christian schools, and attended Bible College, we never once heard anyone speak about sexual abuse, not once. We were totally unprepared to deal with what her father had done to her. It never once entered our minds that he should have been prosecuted. That may be hard for some people to understand, but unless we are taught what to do, the reality is that, regrettably, we do nothing. Is it any wonder that people in church have no clue what to do, when abuse comes to their church? Those who are charged to lead God's people are so often perpetuating a culture of ignorance from one generation of Christians to the next. In John 8:32, we are reminded of Christ's words: "you shall know the truth and the truth shall set you free." Only by speaking the truth about all of the ramifications concerning sexual assault and the harm that is caused by it, will the church ever be free from the shame and damage that it causes. Lack of knowledge enslaves, a people, but the truth sets them free.

The church needs to make sure that there are preventative measures in place to help stop abuse. Everyone should understand the importance of recognizing and reporting abuse. Action items such as: background checks on children's workers, windows in classroom doors, policies that require more than one adult with children at all times, and making sure that churches have training each year for their church staff, are some of the minimum requirements that need to be attended to in local churches.

The church needs to understand why it is important to sever all ties with the sexual offender, if they are unrepentant. Church discipline is only as effective as the participation by church and family members. What often happens in these difficult situations is that some of the church members and some of the family members refuse to do the right thing and don't shun the sexual offender, who is not repentant. Consequently, because they are not isolated completely, the discipline is not effective. Keep in mind that most religious sexual offenders are quick to proclaim their remorse, but very few truly are. When someone admits their sin and then blames others for their insidious actions, they are not repentant! When individuals who have been found out, continue to minimize and excuse their actions, they are not repentant. When sexual offenders reject discipline or get angry at the mention of consequences, it would seem evident that they remain unrepentant. Only when an offender has given up all of their defenses and is truly broken and willing to accept their consequences, can there be any progress in bringing about meaningful change in their lives.

Professional and long-term counseling is needed. Most sexual offenders have developed the skills of lying, deceiving, and manipulating so that the average pastor or counselor is misguided if they think they can change a sexual offender. Though both may leave each counseling session pleased with themselves, the fact is that the sexual offender will most likely continue with their deviant behavior of raping and molesting.

Once the convicted sexual offender has done their jail time, they need to be in a specialized, long-term rehabilitation program. To my knowledge there are only a few ministries that offer rehabilitation for sexual offenders. If an offender can legally and safely attend church, that church needs to make sure to set boundaries and mandate that someone will be with the offender and monitoring them at all times.

There are many things a church must accomplish in order for it to be able to say that they have fulfilled their scriptural mandates for dealing with this sin. Most church leaders seem to want to make a quick statement that condemns this evil and then move on to other things. But the task that the church is facing demands diligence and a daily effort until Christ returns for His children. This battle, like all battles, must be fought with vigilance in order to be won. It is time for Christians to come together to engage this fight to protect the children that God has placed in our care.

Let's look at several more passages. Isaiah 10:1-4 says, "Woe to those who decree unrighteous decrees, who write misfortune which they have prescribed, to rob the needy of justice, and to take what is right from the poor of my people, that widows may be their prey, and that they may rob the fatherless. What will you do in the day of punishment and in the desolation which will come from afar? To whom will you flee for help? And where will you leave your Glory? Without me they shall bow down among the prisoners, and they shall fall among the slain. For all this His anger is not turned away, but His hand is stretched out still."

The prophet Isaiah reminds the reader that God is outraged by those who prey on children and the weak and powerless. Does the church really think that God will overlook the fact that for generations, children have been raped and molested by professing believers in Christ and we have done little or nothing to stop it? When God mentions the writing of unrighteous decrees, to rob the needy of justice, I can't help but think of the many thousands of church leaders, missionary board members and board members of other Christian ministries, who have written policies and procedures, to silence the voice of children and their families, who have gone through sexual abuse. It is happening right now in churches, Christian organizations, and mission boards across the country and God is outraged! If you have been sexually assaulted and you feel like God doesn't care and somehow overlooks what this evil person has done to you, please read and hear what God is saying to offenders and enablers in these verses. "They will be among the slain" and even that will not appease his anger over what the policymakers have done to deprive you of justice. God admonished Israel over and over in the book of Jeremiah, to repent, but they would not and they paid a heavy price. But right up until the end, the false prophets were sure that God's blessing would soon be restored and they tried to silence any voice like Jeremiah's, who called for repentance. Many churches are doing the same thing today. Judgment is near and we continue playing church as though there was nothing wrong, and it would seem that there are few who are truly willing to do an honest assessment of the evil that has crept into so many churches. Proverbs 29: 27 says "an unjust man is an abomination to the righteous, and he who was upright in the way is an abomination to the wicked." If that is true, and of course it is, then why are so many church leaders in bed with those who rape and molest children? We are left with no choice, but to conclude that many of our church leaders are in fact, wicked themselves, otherwise how do we explain this verse. We hear reports of many pastors and missionary boards that are still protecting offenders. An offender's actions should be so odious to us that we are compelled to hold them accountable. According to this verse what the offenders are doing should be an abomination to the righteous. To protect that which is evil, is in fact to be evil.

In Proverbs 31:4-5 the writer says, "…It is not for Kings to drink wine, nor for princes intoxicating drink; lest they drink and forget the law, and pervert the justice of all the afflicted." In this verse God is warning of the dangers of drinking and how it causes someone to forget what is right and thereby pervert the justice of the afflicted. Our church leaders may not be drinking and may not be drunk but many of them are still perverting the justice of the afflicted. I'm sure that most of our church leaders would quickly agree with the dangers of drinking. So the question is, if it is not drunkenness that is causing so many to ignore the plight of the abused, then what is it? Regardless of the cause, the result is the same; the abused are deprived of justice. How many offenders are there, that should be sitting in jail, and are right now preaching in churches or serving as missionaries or being honored as someone who has been a great help to the church? I know that sounds cynical, but the truth is that there are many reports of offenders in all three of these categories. There was a story that came out a few days ago where a church called a pastor back to the pulpit after he was found guilty of molesting two young girls. There are many Christians and churches who are trying to deal with this issue, but much more remains to be done.

As Solomon viewed his world he saw a great deal of injustice and says in Ecclesiastes 3:16, "moreover I saw under the sun, in the place of judgment, wickedness was there and in the place of righteousness, iniquity was there." Faith and I have talked with two ladies who are now in their forties. They attended the same church as teenagers. They were both molested by one of the deacons and when their parents found out as well as with a number of the church leaders, absolutely nothing was done. They simply tried to keep the girls out of his reach. Have you ever truly stopped to ponder the condition of our churches in God's eyes? Eli's two sons were committing adultery and rape in the temple, as the people lined up to come in to sacrifice and worship. We have heard many reports of children being molested within a church building. One pastor told me that a young woman, who began attending his church, had told him and his wife about being molested by an older teen for many years. This had happened while she was attending another church. This was happening in another room, while the church service was going on in the sanctuary. I wonder what God must have felt as the people in the sanctuary prayed for him to bless them and fill the church and prosper their ministry, while the sexual abuse was going on in a nearby room. The people in the church had no idea that she was being sexually abused, but that doesn't change the fact that it was happening. Christians must resist the temptation of taking comfort in the fact that they did not know about a particular instance of abuse. Even if sin is hidden it still has consequences. Being ignorant of something is one thing but being willfully ignorant is another. Most Christians have no idea that sexual assaults are occurring to children that they may know but that is different than Christians who have been exposed to the truth about the subject of sexual abuse and choose to ignore it, that is willful ignorance. The example of Joshua and Israel losing their battle at Ai because of Aachen's sin is an example to the church that even if we don't 'know' about the sexual abuse of children, that doesn't mean there won't be consequences to the local church. Just because people are ignorant of the abuse that may be happening around them does not mean that there will be no collateral damage. They may not be guilty of the sin, but that does not mean that God's blessing will not be removed. We can claim ignorance and hope that God will bless us anyways or we can deal with the sin of sexual abuse and actually have reason to believe that He will bless the Church once again.

Proverbs 28:4 reminds the reader that, "Those who forsake the law praise the wicked, but such as keep the law contend with them." It is not enough for the church and other Christian ministries to simply help the victims. In this passage, the reader is reminded that they are to confront and contend with the offenders and all those who are protecting them. This is not open for debate. The Bible makes this point very clear and God will hold those who disobey accountable for their sin. He expects Christians to defend the abused and contend with the abuser. If we love God's Word, we will take a stand against sexual offenders in the church.

The world is starting to deal with the issue of sexual abuse of children and many in the church are pretending it doesn't happen. How many times did God warn Israel to repent of her sin? They continued to offer their sacrifices and to observe their holy days and fasting, but refused to repent of their sin or even to acknowledge it. Many churches are doing the same thing today. We send out our missionaries and have programs to help the poor and needy. We try to evangelize the world and yet we refuse to repent of our sin or even to acknowledge the abuse that is so rampant, even in our churches.

Let's look at the description of harmful behavior that Paul gives in Romans 1:29-32, ". . . being filled with all unrighteousness, sexual immorality, wickedness, covetousness, maliciousness, full of envy, murder, strife, deceit, evil mindedness, they are whisperers, back biters, haters of God, violent, proud , boasters, inventors of evil things, disobedient to parents, who, knowing the judgment of God, that those who practice such things are deserving of death, not only do the same but also approve of those who practice the same." Our church leaders should know what God's word says about those who abuse children and yet many ignore the evil and refuse to defend the weak and they continue to protect and shelter the offenders.

I had a conversation with a lady who is an enabler to a sexual offender. When I confronted her with her harmful behavior she told me that she did not condone what this man was doing. I had to tell her that by these very actions that she was in fact, condoning what this man was doing, and so are many in the church today. Is it possible to condemn and yet condone something at the same time? When church leaders consistently ignore and minimize the issue, are they by their actions condoning it?

What must the church do to make it right? First, the church must come to a full awareness, as to the extent of this enormous gap in their understanding. Is this gap a sin of omission or commission? Second, the church must confess and repent of its role in the failure to deal with this sin biblically. Third, the church must report abuse to the proper authorities and recognize the government's God given role in these matters. Fourth, the church must become a place of safety for victims. The church body must help victims get the counseling that they need and be prepared to help in any way that they can. The church must recognize that one of the best ways to help victims is to stop the sin and make sure that they seek justice. Fifth, the church must reach out to all those family members of both the victims and the abusers. Sixth, the church must be prepared to help educate the family members, on how they should react to the victims of abuse and what steps they need to take to help them heal. Seventh, the church must understand its responsibility to the offenders, to hold them accountable before God and the law. The church needs to be prepared to exercise church discipline against the offender and they need to be prepared to enforce proper boundaries for those offenders who may be repentant. The church must also understand that even if an offender is repentant, he will need years of in-depth and professional counseling, and will need to have proper boundaries and limitations for the rest of his life. Eighth, the church needs to develop more residential facilities that are designed to help the repentant offenders that have finished their incarceration to find rehabilitation, restoration and forgiveness.

8
The Families' Role in Dealing with Abuse

What is the answer for the family of the victim? What is it that they must do to help their loved ones who have been sexually assaulted? I have dealt with the enablers in an earlier section. For now we are looking at family members who did not know about the abuse and who truly want to get this right. Most of us, when we see someone we love and care for and it is evident that they are hurting, we ask them what can I do to help? Remember that for many women, they are not able to talk about their abuse until much later in life, which complicates the healing process. Victoria Johnson says in her book "Children and Sexual Abuse" "if sexual abuse has occurred, your main concern should be for the victim. If you suspect, or your child reports, a sexual encounter, allow the child to explain what happened. Stay as calm as possible. Don't get angry or blame the child. Believe your child.... rarely do children make up sexual abuse stories."

The first thing the family must do is to make sure the child is in a safe place. This must be done in conjunction with law enforcement. When family members choose not to report the abuse and try to handle it themselves, it only makes the authorities' job more difficult. If they can't trust family members to be honest with the law, they will be very reluctant to trust them with the care of the child who has been abused. When family members report the abuse and cooperate with them, it reassures the authorities that they will be looking out for the child and their safety. When family members know of an offender and take no steps to report them and leave the children in a dangerous situation, the family members can be charged with failure to protect. Remember, that when God tells us in Ephesians 5:11 "to have no fellowship with the unfruitful works of darkness, but rather <u>expose</u> them." He is commanding us to get involved in exposing the evil deeds of offenders. Family members must not sit on the sidelines and hope that somebody else will report their concerns of possible abuse.

We had a woman who came to us a couple of years ago with a tragic story of abuse. She had married a man who seemed to be a wonderful Christian. They had a short engagement, but he appeared to be the model Christian. He owned a home in Florida where his daughter often stayed, and managed to have an excuse as to why his soon-to-be wife shouldn't come to the house. They always went to his parents' house or her house or her church but never his house. His family members seemed to be nice and were all Christians as well, but they were all hiding a very ugly secret. Once they were married and moved into his house, his wife began to suspect that something was terribly wrong with her new husband's relationship with his daughter, who spent more time with her father than with her own husband. The early morning trips to his daughter's bedroom, the sickening feeling that she was a second wife living in the same house. My point in telling this story here is that after she was married to him and living in the same house and in the same town and going to the same church that he had gone to for many years, she was noticing people from his family, church and even from the town coming up to her and mentioning their concern over her new husband's relationship with his daughter. As she was telling us the story, I asked her, how many people had mentioned this to her and she counted at least 12! Think about that for a moment, 12 different people approached his new wife, who thought she had married a godly man, and were bold enough to mention their concern about his relationship with his daughter. It's too bad they didn't have the courage to let her know before the wedding. It is actually likely that if 12 people reported this to her, that there were many more who saw the same thing but said nothing, even his own pastor had concerns, but in public they were a model father and daughter, they would even sing special music as a duet in the church. All of those people had concerns about a very inappropriate relationship. They all saw something was wrong but nobody did a thing, not the pastor, not the family members, not even the church. The new wife had walked into a nightmare believing that God had answered her prayers for a godly husband. Silence continues to allow this evil to go on and on unabated. It seems hard to believe that so many people could see something so wrong and yet do nothing. We've all watched scenes on TV, where somebody is being robbed and people walk by and they see what's happening and they do nothing. We are all horrified that nobody would get involved, that nobody would stop the robbery, nobody would help the victim. The same thing is happening time and time again with sexual abuse. Many people know something is happening and yet they do nothing, nobody protects the victim. Just like the priest and the Levite who walked by the man that was wounded on the road and left for dead. So many Christians are walking by the victims of abuse and doing nothing. If the church does not wake up to what is happening it will have absolutely no credibility left to reach a lost and dying world. Only God knows the whole ugly truth about this father and daughter, but all the evidence points to the fact that he was raping and molesting his daughter and no one would stop him. The father had raised her for many years without a mother in the home and while many people had concerns, no one intervened on her behalf.

If you have concerns about abuse, you have a Biblical mandate to expose the sin, report your concerns to the authorities, and let them do their job. Do you remember the quote, "all that is necessary for evil to triumph, is for good men to do nothing". Every family member should be looking out for the children who are vulnerable. Someone in authority may choose to misuse that authority over them and abuse them. 1 Thessalonians 2:7-11 Paul says, "But we were gentle among you, just as a nursing mother cherishes her own children… as you know, how we exhorted and comforted and charged every one of you, as a father does his own children". Paul describes his relationship with the folks at the church in Thessalonica, as being like that of the caring mother and devoted father. What kind of mother turns a deaf ear to her child when they tell her that something happened to them? What kind of a father rebukes their child, who has come to him for protection from another family member or family friend who is abusing them? If a mom or dad refuses to protect their child then they have failed to do what God has entrusted them to do, their most basic responsibility is to protect, love, and provide for their children. Psalms 27: 10 says" when my father and my mother forsake me, then the Lord will take care of me". It's sad to say but there are many Christian mom and dads who have forsaken their children, by not believing their stories of abuse or by not responding to them. We have talked to many parents whose children no longer talk with them because they felt their parents failed to protect them, and failed to hear their cries for help. We had a mom come to us whose young son had been molested by an older cousin, when she went to her husband with this information to get him to help her deal with the situation, he said it was no big deal and was irritated that she thought it should be dealt with.

We have heard from many victims who have told us that when they told their mother what their father had been doing to them; that he was touching them, she would scold them angrily calling them names which only added to their pain and confusion. Family members must start getting it right by being there for their children when there is abuse and by getting the rest of the family around the child to form a circle of protection.

So one of the first things family members must do is to protect their children. One of the reasons that children are so vulnerable is that there is often a disconnect between the children and the adults in a family. We must have healthy communication with our children if we're going to be able to protect them. Patrick Crough says in his book *The Serpents Among Us* "Because many of us must be employed outside the home, we spend the majority of our day away from our children. Therefore we must make it a point to communicate with our children every day to learn what is going on in their lives and who they are having daily contact with." The family must always protect their children from abuse, but when abuse does occur, the family especially needs to love and support the child as well as seek justice for them.

The second thing we must do is to allow the victim to tell their story. Too often we cut the victim off because we're uncomfortable listening to such an offense. We are in shock and we are sickened while we are being told, but we must allow them to talk, when they are ready. The family can encourage a victim to talk, but they should not try and force them to. Allow them time and space, and always assure them that you are available when they are ready. It is selfish for a family member to say, I don't want to talk about it. That is what Faith's mom has told her and to this day she refuses to let Faith talk with her about the abuse. What a tragedy that is, Faith's mom could help bring healing into Faith's life and could be a great encouragement if she would only take the time to listen and show remorse and compassion for all that she has been through. The abuse was not mom's fault, but she spent much of her time out of the house, as her job was the main source of income for the family. When mom first found out about the abuse, she failed to protect Faith from her dad.

When the family finds out about abuse, they must get the child to a place of safety and don't leave that decision, of whether or not to go, up to the child. That is unfair to them as they are too fragile to know what is best. They also have a moral obligation to report this crime to the proper authorities. Don't pass the buck when it comes to reporting. Sometimes family members will tell a pastor or someone else first, hoping that the pastor will report the abuse, so they don't have to. If the family is finding out about the abuse years later, that specific abuse may be beyond the statute of limitations and the law may not be able to prosecute that case, but you should always report. The laws are different in each state; some states have no statute of limitations on sex abuse crimes. Sometimes there may be circumstances that will allow for prosecution even though it is many years later. If the victim is mentally handicapped it may be possible to prosecute even if it is past the statute of limitations. Even if this particular case is past the statue limitations, the victim and family members should report it for a number of reasons. Because most offenders have many victims, you may be able to help prosecute the offender on a more recent case, by being a witness. It also alerts the authorities to the fact that this person is an offender, and that could be of help in future cases. It also sends a warning to the offender that they have been reported and are being watched by the law and the family.

A woman told us that when her mother died she called her children together and told them that they were no longer to have any contact with her father, because he had raped and molested her for many years. They were all shocked, because they had no idea that their mom had been abused. She had said nothing because she didn't want to hurt her mom, and while that is noble, it still allows others to be in danger. When someone finds out that a family member has been abused, they need to form a protective circle of family members around them. From the many victims that have talked to us about their stories, we have heard that family members often turn against the victim, yelling and screaming, blaming them for the embarrassment and the pain and for the turmoil in the family. I remember the night when Faith's mom called our house around midnight; she was screaming at Faith and asking her when this was going to stop. She was blaming her daughter for the turmoil in the family, not her husband who was doing the raping and molesting… go figure.

Many families and churches are getting much of this issue wrong. Rather than protecting the ones who have been harmed, they are venting at them and unloading their guilt and anger on the victims. In almost all of our conferences and speaking engagements in churches, we have someone ask us "why don't victims report the abuse". There are many reasons, but one of them is that they are further abused and rejected by their own.

Thirdly, the family must protect the child that has been abused. This involves physical protection by making sure the offender cannot have access to the child. You would think that this would be common sense but we have been appalled at the recklessness of family members who seem to think that "Uncle Joe" is really not a bad guy even though he raped and molested one of the children in the family, "after all he is fun to be around and helps people out when they need him". We are familiar with a case where the offender was convicted of molesting a young girl in his family and was not supposed to have any contact with the children and is listed as a registered sex offender. The family was split over the issue, with a great deal of anger and resentment toward the children who took a stand and chose to obey God's word and hold him accountable for his sin. But some of the family invited the offender for a birthday party for one of the grandchildren and they allowed this man, who had raped and molested many children, to sit with their children and even hug them! In their pride, and stubbornness they endangered their own children. While this is outrageous behavior, it is normal in most family situations for some to refuse to protect their children from the offender.

Another way that family members put their children at risk is to try to keep the family secret quiet, because they don't want to talk about it and they don't want to be bothered by it. Faith and I were talking with a lady, not long ago, who had a father-in-law, who was molesting one of his grandchildren and had pled guilty to the charges. She was unaware of what had happened for over five years! Most of the family knew about the abuse and yet they refused to tell the rest of the family. This allows the offender to continue to have access to unsuspecting family members. We couldn't believe that she didn't know, but the reason is that everybody tries to keep the truth from getting out for fear of their own embarrassment. It is time for family members to be more concerned about the safety of their children, than what people will think about them. Remember that Jesus said, "You shall know the truth and the truth shall set you free". When people don't know the truth they cannot protect their children. In other words, ignorance puts children in danger but arming the family with the truth about an offender will help to keep them safe. Jesus says in Matthew 18: 10 "take heed that you do not despise one of these little ones, for I say to you that in heaven their angels always see the face of My Father, who is in heaven". I want you to truly consider what Jesus is saying in this verse. First of all He is giving a serious warning to anyone who despises a child. The Greek word that is translated "despise" means to "think against". Webster says the word despise means to "look down on with contempt, to regard as negligible or worthless." God is talking to all of us and saying that we should not despise or look down on or regarded as worthless, any child. Offenders do not love their victims. You cannot love and destroy the precious life of a little child at the same time. When somebody refuses to help a child who has been abused, they are in effect saying that they are worthless. If Jesus said we will give an account for every idol word, how is it that so many believers think they will not have to answer for the unspeakable acts they commit against children, whether it is the offenders who do the raping and molesting, or the family members who cover it up, or the church members who look the other way. Think about the picture that God paints in this verse; every child has an angel who is beholding God's face. The angel, like most moms and dads, is protective of these precious children and stands before God the Father on behalf of every child. What is it that Jesus is saying to the adults of His day? It certainly is a warning because He tells them "take heed" not to despise a child. Then He threatens them with the knowledge that each child has an angel who is standing in God's presence. The implication is that if you harm this child, you will pay a severe price. If all of this will happen to someone who despises a child, what in the world do we think will happen to someone who rapes or molests a child? We will deal more with this later in the chapter 'Truth'.

The answer for the family is that we are also to be protectors of the children. This means we must be proactive in helping to prevent abuse as well as active in helping children who have been abused to be safe. Far too often our children are not our priority…. we worry about our job, our home, our cars, and everything else under the sun, but not our children. We often take them for granted. Patrick Crough advises in his book "Be aware that the enemy wants parents to place more priorities ahead of their children, thereby placing them in a position where they must rely on other people and resources to care for them." In other words when we don't make our children one of our top priorities, we are putting them at risk.

When it is too late to prevent the abuse and the family is already broken, we must remember that true healing can only come through Jesus Christ and His love for us. It was His sacrifice on the cross that made it possible for us to be forgiven and it is only through Him that we can find the strength to get through this kind of situation. So be a protector not a pretender. A protector sees the danger and comes to the aid of the child. The pretender chooses to ignore the obvious and closes their eyes and ears to the cries of the children and pretends that everything is all right.

9

The Victims' Role in Dealing with Abuse

What is the answer for victims? What happens when the unthinkable happens? How can someone ever recover from the horrific experience of sexual assault? Questions that victims may ask are: Does Jesus care? Does He see? Where was God when I was being abused? Will I ever be whole again? Will I ever be able to be married? Will I ever be able to enjoy sex with my future husband or wife?

They Must Understand God's Love for Them

The questions for the victims are many and are often overwhelming. I was not a victim of abuse, therefore in this chapter I will draw from the years that I have spent with my wife and the many stories and testimonies that have been shared with us, as well as to look into God's Word and consider what He has to say. It cannot be stressed enough that the first step to healing begins with receiving Jesus Christ as your Lord and Savior. Most victims feel that they are unlovely, without value, guilty, and even unworthy, but Jesus said in John 3:16: "For God so loved the world that He gave His only begotten son, that whoever believes in Him should not perish but have everlasting life." Every person is so important to God that He sent His dear Son to die for them. Each person is so valuable to God that He made a way for people to know Him. God wants you with Him for eternity so much so that He died for you. God did not die for a bunch of good people, but He died for sinners, people who were broken, lost, hurting and in desperate need of Him.

When you ask yourself the question, "Where was God when I was being abused?" say to yourself, "He was on the cross." Even though Jesus hung on the cross on a day almost 2000 years ago, He endured the pain and suffering because of His love for you right now. What happened to you was not right and God is outraged with the one who has harmed you. But never forget that Jesus didn't deserve what He received on the cross. Jesus never did anything wrong, and yet He was beaten and scorned. His flesh was torn by whips, the crown of thorns was placed on His head and then they hit His head with a rod, driving the crown of thorns deep into His scalp, His body was so weakened that He didn't have the strength to carry His own cross. When they reached the place where He was crucified they drove the nails into His hands and feet, then they stood the cross up, where He hung until He died. Remember when Jesus said in John 12:32 "and I if I be lifted up from the earth, will draw all people to myself". Jesus desires that His sacrifice for you on the cross will draw you to Him, and just as He rose on the third day, He wants to bring peace and love into your life and to have you with Him for eternity. He desires to transform you out of the suffering and pain into a new life, a real life. Jesus said that He has come to bring new life and that more abundantly.

For the child who has been abused, their world is turned upside down. God has given to everyone a sense of right and wrong. Even a young child knows that it is wrong to steal, kill or lie. A child also knows that what has been done or continues to be done to them is not right. They may be confused about who was to blame, since most sexual offenders will either blame the victim or someone else for what is happening. To the child, it may seem like nobody loves them, even their mom and dad. Even in cases where the parents are not the abusers the child feels like they have not been protected by their parents and will take that to mean that they do not care about what is happening to them and that they do not love them.

Many people who have gone through sexual abuse also feel that God does not love them or else He would have stopped the sexual assaults. The first part of the answer for the victims is that they must come to know that God does truly love them. That is seen in the story of the cross and the incredible sacrifice that God made for them. How many times have we, as parents, found ourselves trying to explain to our children that we love them? Often it is a situation where our children are angry or hurt over something we did or something we won't let them do and they feel that we don't love them. God wants the person, who has gone through abuse to know that He does love them.

Jeremiah was a prophet of God in the Old Testament and God told him in Jeremiah 1:5 that "before I formed you in the womb, I knew you, before you were born, I sanctified you, I ordained you a prophet to the nations." God had an amazing plan for Jeremiah's life, but that doesn't mean that everything was pleasant. Most of the people that God sent him to did not like what he had to say. God sent him to warn the people about their sin and the need to repent. He was only a youth when God first called him and there were many times that his life was in danger. But the lowest point in his life came when he was placed in a dungeon in the king's palace. The Bible says that when they put him in the dungeon he "sank in the mire." The bottom of the dungeon was filled with mud and filth so deep that he literally sank to the depth that he could not move. He was surely going to face an agonizing death of starvation and suffering. He was hated by most, he was mocked and ridiculed and left to die in the stink and darkness of the dungeon.

Sometimes that is how we feel in life. For the child who has been sexually abused it seems like no one cares and the abuse leaves them in shame and darkness. It feels like a dungeon they will never be able to escape from. Like those who have been sexually abused, Jeremiah felt that God had betrayed him. After all, God had told Jeremiah that He had chosen him to be a prophet to the nations. If that was true, why was he in a dungeon, buried in the mire, and running out of time? In fact, Jeremiah had suffered so much at the hands of the very people he was trying to help. He said in chapter 20 "then I said I will not make mention of Him or speak in His name anymore." This did not last very long, since Jeremiah found that God's Word was powerful within him. He says it this way: "His word was in my heart like a burning fire, shut up in my bones and I was weary with holding it back, and I could not hold back any longer." Jeremiah did not understand why God would allow these things to happen, especially if He called him to be a prophet for Him. It just did not make sense! There are many things in this life that don't make sense, like a child being raped or molested by someone who professes to be a Christian. And like Jeremiah, many people who have been sexually assaulted decide that if God will not protect them from the evils of this world, then they don't want to serve Him.

Jeremiah knew in his heart, that only God truly had the answers to the sin and evil of this world. So too, with the victims of abuse, they need to remember that God really does love them and He is the one that they need most. Jesus told his disciples in John 15:13 that, "Greater love has no man than this, that he would lay down his life for his friends". Not long after Jesus said these words He went out and did just that, He gave His life for us. You must understand God's love for you.

They need to see themselves as God sees them

How does God see the child who has gone through the excruciating experience of sexual assault one time or a number of times? Genesis 16 contains a tragic story in many ways. It is the story of how two godly people go outside God's will for their lives and cause a tremendous amount of pain in the lives of others. God had promised Abraham and Sarah that they would have a child and that God would cause their descendants to become a great nation one day. Sarah was well past childbearing years and it seemed like God's promise had failed. So Sarah came up with an idea that seemed logical to her. She told her husband to take her servant girl, named Hagar, and he could have a child by her. Hagar was forced into a relationship with someone, so that he could have sex with her and produce a child that Sarah could claim as her own. While it was common in those days for men to have more than one wife and while slavery was common in those days, it does not make what they did, right—because Sarah did not trust what God had said about them as a couple having a child of their own. This was never God's plan for Abraham and Sarah.

My purpose in telling the story here is because of what happens next. After the child was born Hagar now has a prestige that holds some weight against her mistress. Since Hagar has borne a child, and especially a son, when Sarah could not, now Hagar despises Sarah. The animosity between Sarah and Hagar was so great that Sarah dealt 'harshly' with her servant. Sarah treats her so badly that Hagar is forced to flee from their home. The Bible says that Hagar took the child and went into the wilderness--not knowing what to do or where to go. At her lowest point and in the moment of her deepest need, God met her and spoke to her. God told her that her son would be a great nation one day and that the Lord has heard her affliction. I want you to notice that God acknowledges her affliction. She had been abused, mistreated, and rejected by Sarah and Abraham, but her suffering was noticed by God. Victims often think that they are alone and that no one knows or cares about their abuse. But God does know and He does care.

What Hagar says next is very important. She declares that God is "the God who sees." She realized that God saw her--in her pain, in her suffering, and in her loneliness. She realized that God was meeting her where she was at. The victim must see themselves as God sees them. Hagar may very well have expected to die there in the wilderness since she was a slave girl far from home who felt completely alone without love or compassion. But that is not what God saw. He was compassionate towards her in her distress and He cared for her a great deal. God was gracious to her and gave her hope by telling her that her son would become a great nation one day. God saw Hagar as someone who was precious and of great value and He came down to her on her level, spoke kindly to her, and reassured her that He had a plan for her life.

God sees value in you, so much so that He was willing to pay the ultimate price so that you could live forever with Him. He gave His life for you. God shows you how much He values you. Many victims see themselves as 'damaged goods'. We have people share with us that this is how they see themselves. Their offenders would tell them that no one would love them or that no one would want to be married to them. This is one of the many insidious ways that sexual offenders continually beat down their victims and keep them enslaved. All of us are like broken vessels, but God can make us whole again, no matter what we have been through.

There is a passage in Ezekiel 8:12 which gives us some insights into God's ability to see in places where people think he can't see: "God said to me, have you seen what the elders of the house of Israel do in the dark, every man in the room of his idols? For they say, the Lord does not see us." The religious leaders of that time thought that God had forsaken Israel and that He would not see all the evil that they were doing in the darkness. The religious, sexual offenders have somehow convinced themselves that God does not see what they are doing to the children, but of course God does see. He is 'the God who sees', just like Hagar said. God sees the children who have been sexually abused and He sees you and what you have suffered and He will one day deal with your offender. God has His eye on them as well.

In the book of I Samuel 16:7 we read this thought: "man looks on the outward appearance but the Lord looks on the heart." People have a tendency to only see the outward which is broken, the hurt, and the damaged. Most of us have gone to see a loved one after an accident or major surgery and we cringe at their appearance. Their body is swollen, they have scars and the signs of the trauma that they have been through are obvious. The victim of sexual abuse often sees themselves in much the same way. They see the ugliness of the abuse and the damage. They often do not like how they see themselves and can even grow to hate themselves. The child who has been sexually violated must come to see themselves as God sees them, as someone who is fearfully and wonderfully made. David says in Psalms 139 that people are a marvelous creation, and that God was involved in every detail of how they were made. Individuals, men and women, boys and girls are special in God's sight no matter how they feel or how they think that they look on the outside. People were created in the image of God and his people are precious to him.

Hagar was rejected by those who should have been caring for her and became an outcast, but she was not forgotten by God. Even though she was not a part of God's plan for Sarah and Abraham's descendants, God had a plan for her and her son. People who have been through abuse often feel that they don't fit in and that life is over for them. There are children that are born as a result of rape and they are trying to understand, who they are and how they fit into God's plan. This can be very difficult. Faith and I spoke at a college a couple of years ago and a young man came up to us afterwards and said: "I am a product of that" meaning abuse. His mother had been raped, as a teenager, by a Christian worker at a home for troubled teens. He was having a real struggle with his identity and just how he fit into this world.

We've had people share with us that their parents would tell them that they were a mistake. I don't know if the parents realize how much damage they do to their children when they say things like this. The pain, hurt, and confusion is unbearable and can last their whole life. There are no mistakes with God. People sin, yes that's true, and many children are born at a time when mom and dad have not planned for them. But no child is an accident in God's eyes.

The survivor of abuse or the child that is born out of sexual assault is loved by God and has been given a special purpose in life, just like everyone else. Think about Hagar and Ishmael again. Hagar had no say in what Abraham and Sarah decided. She was a slave girl and after she was pregnant and Sarah deals harshly with her, she has to flee into the wilderness to escape the mistreatment. While Hagar does return, thirteen years later she has to flee again. It is clear that this was not a part of God's plan. So was Ishmael an outcast in God's eyes or was Hagar contemptible in God's eyes? No not at all. As a matter of fact God tells her that she would bear a son and that God would bless him and make his descendants into a great nation one day. When God sees you, he doesn't just see what has happened to you but He sees you for who you are as a person and He knows the plans that He has for you. Everyone who has gone through sexual abuse needs to see themselves from God's perspective and the best way to do that, once you have accepted Christ the savior, is to spend time in God's Word.

They Must See God For Who He Is

The survivor must get a glimpse of who God is in order to put everything into perspective. The trials, tribulations, and sufferings of this life are only temporary for the believer in Christ. Paul said in Romans 8:18 "for I consider that the sufferings of this present time are not worthy to be compared with the Glory which shall be revealed in us." God is not making light of our sufferings. He is trying to get us to look at our sufferings in light of eternity. This life usually lasts less than 100 years, but eternity is forever, and all pain and suffering will be forgotten. In Revelations 21:4, we read "and God will wipe away every tear from their eyes, there shall be no more death, nor sorrow, nor crying. There shall be no more pain, for the former things are passed away." There is a song titled "Our God is in Control". The first line starts "When our vision of God is small, our problems seem great in size." Those who have suffered enormously especially need to see just how great God is. I think one of the places in the Bible that brings this out is the book of Job. The story starts out with things going very well for Job. He is wealthy, has a large family with many flocks in herds, and he loves the Lord. For many victims, life may seem to start out well with the early years of their childhood even being happy years with a sense of love and security. Then their life is shattered by sexual abuse. In many cases, their sexual abuse may last for the rest of their childhood. Sometimes their sexual abuser may continue to rape and molest them well into their adult years. By this time the victim is so demoralized that they feel completely helpless to try to change their circumstances. They are afraid of their offender and have given up hope for a better or a normal life.

Job's world was shattered in one day. The Bible says that Satan set in motion a series of events that would rob Job of everything he possessed, along with the tragic death of his ten children. Job's world came crashing down around him and no one except his wife knew the intense pain and heartache that he felt. These things did not happen to Job because of his sin. We read, in both chapters one and two of the Book of Job that Job was a godly and an upright person. Satan desired to destroy

Job's testimony, but God allowed the suffering in his life, because in the end, it would be an opportunity for Job to glorify God. At first Job's reaction is amazingly controlled and disciplined. He praises God and acknowledges His authority over his life. Then Satan assaults him with yet another attack. He afflicts him with a grievous illness and his whole body is covered in painful and putrid sores that were so bad, that he could not even stand on his feet, but sat on an ash heap outside of his home. His friends, family, and acquaintances forsook him. Though many once had great admiration for him, when his trials came, they turned away from him. If that wasn't difficult enough, Job had three friends who got together and decided to try and come to visit him, in order to comfort him. When they arrived, they were in shock at how severe Job's condition was. They sat in silence at first.

Job finally cried out in his pain and agony and cursed the day he was born and expressed the grief that he felt. His friends were taken back by his words and quickly tried to tell Job why all this had happened to him. They assumed that Job had done something very wrong and that if he would just repent of all the things he had done wrong, that God would fix everything. His so called friends then took turns debating with him. They provoked Job to say a lot of things that he probably would not otherwise have said. Eventually Job got around to questioning why God had brought all the suffering into his life. He pointed out to God, that He did not have a good reason for doing this, because he had done nothing wrong or deserving of such evil circumstances. Job went on to say that he wished God would give him an audience so that he would lay out his case before Him. Job would show God that there was no justifiable reason for all of this heartache to have befallen him.

I want to use Job's story because there are many parallels between his story and with what happens in the life of someone who is sexually assaulted as a child. It is not the sin of the child that causes the sexual abuse to happen. It is because of the evil of the perpetrator and because of sin in the world in general. We live in a sinful and fallen world, a world where horrible things happen to many people every day. There have been times in history when God has intervened, and there are times when He does so today. Though God answers prayers, does miracles, and works in people's lives every day, He does not exempt us from the trials and the afflictions of life. God provides Christians with spiritual armor in order to stay standing and He wants his people to trust Him no matter what comes their way. But He does not stop the attack of the enemy. After many chapters of Job's pleading with God to give him an answer, as to why all this has happened to him, to Job's great surprise, God appears to speak with him personally. It would seem that finally Job was going to get some answers, as to why these things had happened and if he had done something wrong or how he had brought all this on himself. At least Job would finally know. But that is not what happened. Instead God talked about Himself and how amazing all of creation was. He never once mentions what had happened to Job. For four chapters God talks about creation. He talked about His wisdom and power and how He created and fashioned the whole earth. In chapter 38, God starts out telling Job that He was going to question him, and asks Job if he knows how He made the world? The Creator God then talked about the clouds and the water. He talked about gravity and how it affects the oceans. He talked about the sunrise and the gates of death. He talked about the springs at the bottom of the oceans and the treasury of snow and hail. He talked about lightning and thunder.

In chapter 38:36 we read one of God's many questions to Job. He asked: "Who has put wisdom in the mind?" God talked about mankind's minds and hearts and the fact that He has created wisdom and understanding. In other words, God invented the genetic code, He created DNA as the building blocks of all life forms. In all of chapter 39 God talked to Job about the animal kingdom and all the amazing things that He designed and created in animals--from their strength, beauty, majesty, and grace to their cunning and speed. In chapters 40 and 41, believe it or not, God talked about two of the most awesome creatures that He ever made. They were two dinosaurs; one was called behemoth and the other leviathan. Then He described in detail their amazing size, strength, and their supremacy on both land and the sea.

For four chapters God never mentions what Job had gone through; for four chapters, God answers none of Job's primary questions. God took Job's attention off of his own problems and put it on God's greatness. To someone who has gone through sexual abuse or great pain and suffering, you may actually find God's response to Job offensive, but before you judge God, I want you to hear what Job had to say. In chapter 42, we read: "Then Job answered the Lord and said, 'I know that you can do everything and that no purpose of yours can be withheld from you. You asked 'who is this that darkens council without knowledge?' Therefore I have uttered what I did not understand, things too wonderful for me, which I did not know. Listen, please and let me speak, you said 'I will question you and you shall answer me'. Then Job said 'I have heard of you by the hearing of the ear. But now my eye sees you, therefore I abhor myself and repent in dust and ashes."

Even though Job did not get any of his questions answered, what God said to Job changed his life. Job was completely transformed from being hurt, angry, and confused to seeing who God really is. He gets a glimpse of God for the first time in his life. Even if God were to give you a reason or an answer as to why you have gone through abuse, it would not take away the pain and the longing that you have inside. The only thing that will help transform your life and give it meaning, purpose, and peace is for you to see God for who He is. When we truly see how great God is, it will help the sufferings in this life seem less in comparison and as we contemplate eternity with Him, it will help us to endure what happens on earth.

They Must Understand Their Identity in Christ

In Ezekiel 16:1-6, God described the condition of Jerusalem as a newborn baby who had been abandoned and left for dead. It had not been washed or clothed, and the umbilical cord had not been cut. No one pitied the child or lifted a hand to help, but God came along and loved the baby that had been despised, neglected, and abandoned. He carefully washed the baby and clothed and cared for it. Often, the child who has been abused only sees their own brokenness. And, in many ways they have been abandoned and rejected by the people who should have been caring for them. The truth is that everyone is in a state of brokenness and uncleanness before they accept Christ as their Savior.

We Are His New Creation

The survivor will need to take the time to deal with their abuse and its ramifications in their life. There will be many times that they will need to reference their past for various reasons, but the primary focus needs to shift away from the past abuse to their new life in Christ. Wendy Maltz says in her book *The Sexual Healing Journey*,(pg 29) "Acknowledging past sexual abuse is an important step in sexual healing." When we accept Christ as our Savior, so many things change in our lives. We are encouraged by the passage in 2 Cor. 5:17 which says, "Old things are passed away and behold all things are become new." That is not talking about something that will happen in the future, it is talking about what takes place when individuals receive Jesus into their life now. People are no longer condemned, broken sinners, but become children of the King. People are then adopted and baptized into the family of the One who created the heavens and the earth.

While an individual's standing before God completely changes, many of life's circumstances have not. Individuals still live in a physical body, suffer pain and discouragement, and with the effects of sin that have not yet been lifted from this earth. People become entirely clean and new on the inside because they have been made alive spiritually but they reside for now in a fleshly body that is subject to decay. That is why it is hard to picture our new standing in Christ—although it can be seen by faith, the eye, still sees the evident brokenness. Nevertheless one day soon that will all change. The one who loves and knows Christ as Savior and Friend will receive all that God has promised them through Christ. A good illustration of this is the thief on the cross. One of the thieves, who were crucified with Jesus, spoke up and acknowledged his sin and that Jesus was Lord. He boldly asked Jesus to remember him when Christ came into His kingdom and Jesus replied "Today you will be with me in paradise." In that moment of time the thief's standing before God changed and he had God's promise of eternal life. His physical circumstances did not immediately change. He was still hanging on a cross in agony waiting for his physical life to come to an end.

For the one who has been abused there is hope for healing and restoration in this life. God tells us in 2 Cor. 5:17 that "Old things are passed away and behold all things are become new". When we become a child of God, He makes us 'new'. Some of that 'newness' is immediate and some 'newness' grows with time. When Faith began her healing process, she began to grow into the person that God had intended her to be all the time. But the complete transformation will take place once we are in heaven. Rev. 21:5 "then He who sat on the throne said, behold I make all things new." God can and will make all things new, whether it is in this life or eternity.

We Are His Beloved Child

There were a number of occasions during Jesus' ministry when He took little children up in His arms and blessed them. He also took each of these opportunities to teach the disciples important lessons about God's love for children. In Matthew 18:10, Jesus said, "take heed that you do not despise one of these little ones, for I say to you that in heaven, their angels always see the face of My Father, who was in heaven." In this verse we see Jesus holding a child and saying that their angels always behold the face of My Father. This verse seems to teach that every child has an angel. Perhaps every child has their own angel or perhaps there is one that specifically acts on behalf of all the children, but in either case God has appointed an angel to watch over what is happening to every child. God loves them, He embraces them and He cares for them. It is God's desire that everyone would become a child of God and be a part of His family. 11 Peter 3:9 says, "The Lord is not slack concerning His promise, as some men count slackness, but as long suffering toward us, not willing that any should perish, but that all should come to repentance".

   I remember when our five children were little, one of my favorite things to do was to hold them and have them put their arms around my neck or put their head on my shoulder, it was the most special feeling of love and being loved--that is how it is with God. Now I have two grandsons and I enjoy the same moments with them. God loves us and wants us to love Him back. That may very well be the reason He made us in the first place. A passage in the Book of Psalms reminds us that, "as a father pities his children, so the Lord pities those who fear him." (103: 13). 'Fear' in this verse has the idea of a 'respect' or 'reverence' for God. For the person who has been sexually abused by a parent, this verse may be hard to picture or understand, when God is saying that He pities us as a loving parent would pity their own children. What is pity? To me it means that when my children are hurting, that I am also hurting inside for them. There have been many nights that I have gone to bed crying because my children were hurting. There are times when we can help our children through their aches and pains, and there are times when we are powerless to do anything to help, and we can only be there and hope that our presence will bring a measure of comfort. While God is all powerful, He often chooses to simply be with us and help us get through a trial, rather than stopping it from happening. There were a number of times when Jesus wept, and on each of those occasions it was over the hurts that others were going through. Jesus wept over Jerusalem and the people who have lived there over the centuries and how He had desired to protect them and how they so often turned away from God. Jesus wept when his friend Lazarus died. When he saw the grief of Lazarus' family after he had passed away, Jesus was moved with compassion. Like the loving parent who picks up their child off the ground, after they have fallen and skinned their hands and knees, and torn their clothes, and they shed a tear for the hurt that their child is going through. So God holds people close and sheds a tear for the pain and torment of a child who has been sexually abused.

We Are Called By His Name

Every child bears the name of their parents. When someone accepts Christ as their Savior, they are called by His name. The term 'Christian' was first used to refer to believers in the early church in the city of Antioch. Whether it is the name Christian or Child of God, when we receive Christ as our Savior, we are a part of the family of God and we bear His name. It is a special meaning to give your name to someone. When parents adopt a child, they bring that child into their home and that child becomes their own, they are forever a part of that new family. So when someone, who has gone through abuse, gives their life to Christ, they are called by a new family name--and will have that name for eternity. We are reminded of this fact when we read this verse in the book of John: "but these are written that you may believe that Jesus is the Christ, the son of God and that believing you may have life in His name" (20:31). It is through

Christ's name and faith in His name and what He has done for us on the cross that we are redeemed.

God loves us so much that He brings us into His family and gives us His name. Sadly, for many victims of sexual abuse, their families are angry or offended at them because they think that the victims bring shame and embarrassment to the family name. But God welcomes his children to bear His name. We have gone through this with some in Faith's family and I've heard many stories of others going through the same things. Many families don't want the family name in the paper because others will connect them with whatever happened. But God is happy to embrace those precious children who have suffered through sexual abuse and He welcomes all those who accept Him, to be called by His name, no matter what they have gone through.

We Bear His Image

For many victims, the thought that their families are ashamed of them makes the pain unbearable and a constant wound. But God is not ashamed of our wounds and scars. He is in the process of making us more like Him each day. God created Adam and Eve in His own image. In the book of Genesis 1:26, God says, "let us make man in our own image, according to our likeness." Man's sin has turned God's beautiful creation into something, that at times, is very ugly, but God is in the process of transforming His children into His own image. In the book of 2 Corinthians, the Apostle Paul reminded the Christians there that they were all "being transformed into the same image" of the Living God "by the spirit of the Lord" (3:18). Every mom or dad has a special joy when someone says that their adorable baby looks like them. We feel a sense of pride and identity with this new life. Every new Christian, no matter how wounded or scarred, has not only been adopted into God's family but they also bear His image. Now many times, our life may not be a good representation of who God is, but as we grow in Christ, we will become more and more like Him. The Corinthians were reminded that just as they had "borne of the image of the man of dust [Adam]," that they would "also bear the image of the heavenly man [Christ Jesus]" (I Corinthians 15:49). All people are the descendants of Adam and all people reflect the fallen condition that entered the human race when Adam sinned. When individuals receive Jesus, as their Lord and Savior, they begin to reflect the image of the Son of God, the sinless God-Man. God's desire is that his children: "be conformed to the image of His son" (Romans 8:29). Because God is all knowing, He knew in eternity past, all those who would receive Him as their Savior, and He predestined that each one of them would be conformed to His image. The word 'conformed' means 'jointly formed' or 'similar'. Like jello in a bowl, it takes on the same 'form' or 'image' as the bowl. You may see yourself as broken, unfixable, unlovely, but God sees you as becoming more like Him each day of your Christian life. He sees you as being part of his spiritual family. Do you see the family resemblance? Maybe not yet, but one day, when we are all together in heaven, you will.

We Will Sit Together In Heavenly Places

Sometimes it is hard to see beyond this life on earth with all of its hardships, but this life will soon be over and whether it is through death or the return of Christ at the rapture; God's children will one day step into eternity.

Paul reminded the Ephesian Christians that—they had been made alive spiritually, even though they were naturally among those who were 'dead in trespasses and sins.' All of them had just walked in the way of the broken world, like everyone else, and were influenced by the Evil One, who works through fallen people. God was not going to let this condition continue. Paul reminds them that it was because of God's great love and mercy that he intervened to change their condition. He made them "alive together with Christ," raised them up spiritually, and made them able to "sit together in heavenly places in Christ Jesus." (Eph. 2:1-6) How marvelous is that! This is so amazing and is in such contrast to the place of sin and death that they had been born into, as humans.

I wanted you to be aware of the truths in these verses, so that you can see what Christ has saved his people out of, and where He now has placed us. Verse 6 confirms to Christians today that Christ has raised them up and made them to sit together in heavenly places. Believers in Christ are in an 'official' sense--sitting with Christ in heaven. This also affirms that Christians are already citizens of heaven. For children who have endured sexual abuse, there are people who don't want to be around you, because it may make them feel uncomfortable, but Jesus has already placed you in heaven next to Him! How wonderful it will be when we are truly physically there with Him! Jesus, Himself is looking forward to that day when you will be with Him. Have you received Him as your Lord and Savior?

Paul goes on to say in verse 7, that in the ages to come, God might "show the exceeding riches of His grace in His kindness toward us in Christ Jesus." Not only is the Father and the Son looking forward to you being with them in heaven, but God will shower his people with kindness for all of eternity. The abuse will be long forgotten, the rejection, the humiliation, the nightmares will never again come into your mind, but you will enjoy being with Jesus, along with all of God's children forever. People who love God are encouraged to:

"Look for new heavens and a new earth in which righteousness dwells." (2 Peter 3:13). This is the hope of all who love the God who sent His son Jesus to help them in their dilemma in this life.

10
The Offender's Role in Dealing with Abuse

This is perhaps the most difficult section of this book. What are the answers for offenders? Can they be forgiven? Can they ever be trusted again? Will everything go back to normal? Do they have to leave the ministry? How do we know they are truly repentant?

In our 'Speaking Truth in Love' presentations, we use the results of different studies to show the extent of this sin. One study indicates that the average offender rapes or molests as many as 117 victims. Another statistic from one of the studies shows that offenders had an average of 51 victims before being caught for the first time. If that is true, in most cases the average offender is entrenched in this evil lifestyle and it makes it extremely difficult to bring them out of it. If it was not for Matthew 19:26, that says, "With men this is impossible, but with God all things are possible", we would be tempted to give up entirely, that there is any real hope for the offender. But Jesus is not referring to offenders in this verse, he is referring to the difficulty of a rich man putting his faith and trust in Jesus for salvation. But the last part of the verse still applies to our use here, "with God of all things are possible". We all have heard the stories of how hard it is to stop an addiction. The alcoholic, who is losing his marriage, his job and his life are falling apart and yet he seems powerless to change, needs intervention. The offender, who rapes and molests children, needs a miracle.

I remember like it was yesterday, hearing the words that Faith's dad had used after he had been caught in his latest molesting of a child. Some of the family and the church were attempting to hold him accountable for his sin and he was doing his usual whining and complaining about how everyone was being mean to him and he told one of the family, "I said I was sorry, what more can I do"? This seems to be a typical response and it reveals the depravity of the one who says it. First of all, saying you are sorry is doing nothing and all. It is a copout, a way to avoid doing anything that is substantive. In this section we will look at what God says needs to happen for there to be forgiveness and the possibility of restoration. I mentioned earlier in the book about the night we went to confront dad with what he had done to Faith's niece. When we walked into his house, he was sitting on the couch with his left hand on an open Bible, he started talking about all that God was teaching him and wanted us to believe that he had already squared things with God and was right with him. This was his way of saying that we didn't have to be involved or report anything to the authorities, because it was all taken care of now. Nothing could have been farther from the truth, he was not right with God nor had he taken any of the steps that are needed in order to get oneself right with God. We will look at five steps that every offender must take before they can make the case that they have done everything necessary to be right with God.

Must find a place of repentance

Repentance means "to turn and go the other way." So how do we know when an offender is repentant? Not when he says he is sorry, not when he sheds a few tears, it is when he turns his life from sin and back to following God. Repentance is not just saying a few words. It is a complete change of heart and behavior. The book of Hebrews 12: 16, 17 says, "lest there be any fornicator or profane person like Esau, who for one morsel of food, sold his birthright." For you know that afterward, when he wanted to inherit the blessing, he was rejected, for he found no place of repentance, though he sought it diligently with tears". The religious offender, who has chosen to rape and molest a child and thinks that they can shed a few tears and then everything will be forgiven and forgotten, is sadly mistaken. Esau was born first and that entitled him to the birthright, which was a larger share of the inheritance and the blessing of his father. Esau had no respect for God's provision and recklessly traded it to Jacob for some food. But when Jacob wound up with the blessing, Esau was angry and bitter and was moved to tears as he pleaded with his father for a blessing. The point is, it was too late, he had despised God's blessing and traded it away.... it was gone. God says in Hebrews 12: 17, "that Esau found no place of repentance even though he sought it with tears". Like Esau, the religious offender lightly esteems his standing before God and recklessly trades away Godliness and a right relationship with Him for a moment of lust, power and control over a helpless child. I believe it is possible for an offender to be able to repent, but it is not guaranteed. From the statistics that we have read and the results of the stories we have heard, it seems that very few offenders ever truly repent. Consider the passage in the book of Hebrews 6: 4-6 "for it is impossible for those who were once enlightened, and have tasted the heavenly gift, and have become partakers of the Holy Spirit, and have tasted the good word of God and the powers of the age to come, if they fall away, to renew them again to repentance, since they crucify again for themselves the Son of God, and put Him to an open shame." The offender, who claims to be a Christian and so despises God that they would harm one of these precious children in this manner, had better be greatly afraid indeed. Most offenders simply brush off what they have done as no big deal, but it is to God and it is to the children whose lives they have so damaged. Bill Anderson says in his book that the person, who had molested the children in his church, seemed to have no idea how much harm he had done to his victims. "When he came into contact with his victims and their families, he seemed to have no comprehension of the emotional distress he was inflicting on them."

It seems to be very difficult for an offender to repent. Enablers will often talk about how sorry offenders are and of course most offenders will claim the same, but from what we have seen, read and heard, many offenders are only sorry that they were caught or they are sorry that their ministry is in jeopardy or that they are being inconvenienced by the victims pursuit of justice. This is not godly sorrow at all, but a discomfort that they disdain having to go through. I believe that any sinner can find this place of repentance, but it comes from a genuine brokenness over what we have done and how it has impacted people's lives. That is why Esau could not find a place of repentance, because his heart was not right, he was angry at missing the blessing but had no remorse for his sin that led to the loss. Offenders and enablers are quick to demand that the victim forgives them and claim that they have repented, but often they lack the very premise necessary to be repentant; a broken heart over their evil and the crimes that they have committed.

If we use David as an example of repentance, we find in Psalms 51 that David, once he was confronted by Nathan the prophet with his sin, was truly broken over it and sought forgiveness, with uncontrollable crying for many days, he went without food because of what he had done, he was very ashamed. With Faith's dad there was no visible shame at all, he would be out in public talking with people as though nothing had happened, he was on the phone with people from our church, telling them that he had done nothing wrong. As I mentioned earlier, he was reportedly at another church singing in their choir, just weeks after he had molested his granddaughter. But David accepted the consequences and took responsibility for what he had done. That laid the foundation for David's Godly repentance. David had committed adultery with his friend's wife and then had his friend killed, and yet David was able to find a place of repentance before God. So what is the difference between David and Esau? David's remorse was over his sin and the damage it caused, Esau's remorse was over what he was missing out on, two completely different things. II Peter 3:9 says "that God is not willing that any should perish but that all should come to repentance." It is God's will that all should find that place of repentance. We had a mother, that called us and told us her husband had molested their daughter several years ago and that when she confronted him, he had repented and was on his knees crying and begging for forgiveness, it seemed real. But the daughter had just recently found a camera in the bathroom where the father had been taking video of her in the shower. Christians are too quick to blindly accept the claim that an offender is repentant. Godly sorrow and true repentance can only be known over time. Matthew 3:7, 8, "And when John saw many of the Pharisees and Sadducees coming to his baptism, he said to them 'brood of vipers! Who warned you to flee from the wrath to come? Therefore bear fruits worthy of repentance.'" The religious offender may be the biggest hypocrite of them all. John commanded the hypocrites of his day to bear fruits worthy of repentance. The offender can only be believed after they have demonstrated a consistent pattern of Godly living and established fruits that are consistent with true repentance. Anything short of that is not repentance and not to be believed. John had no problem calling the religious leaders, 'vipers' and challenging their very motives for being there. Remember that one of the things that was being claimed by those that John was baptizing, was repentance of sins and yet John refused to accept the Pharisees and Sadducees, because it was evident that they were not. Acts 26: 20 says "that they should repent, turn to God, and do works be fitting repentance." Think of this, that even God, who sees the heart and knows for sure that someone is repentant, demands evidence in the life and works of those who claim it.

Yes an offender can repent and can be forgiven, but the road to repentance is not easy and most will try to go around, but only by walking this road will the offender ever be right with God and find forgiveness.

Must Make a True Confession

God's definition of confession is more than just admitting to something. I John 1:9 says that "If we confess our sins, He is faithful and just to forgive us our sins and cleanse us from all unrighteousness". Confess means "to ascent" or "to agree with God about our sin". If confession is only acknowledgment, then someone could confess without being repentant. But if confession means to agree with God, then it is conceivable that one cannot make a true confession without being repentant. The offender must make a full confession of all of their crimes and this must be an open confession before the law, counselors, victims, victim's families and his own family and also the church. In other words, for it to be real, it must be an open confession. This does not mean that literally all these people have to be there but it means that the offender tells the truth to all who ask, not confess to one and lie to another. Without that kind of transparency there truly is no real confession. To try and hide the confession from others is an indicator that the offender still is not ready to own up to his own sin and is not ready to begin the lengthy process of dealing with it. It is important for crime victims to hear their offender confess to what they have done. What happens, many times, is that offenders will acknowledge to a few who already know the truth, but then turn around and lie to others and deny the truth. This is not a confession. We as God's children must insist that offenders make a true and full confession and that they be consistent in telling the truth. In the book of Ephesians 5: 16 it says, "confess your trespasses to one another". When an offender lies to someone about what they have done, they cannot be believed in anything that they claim. To tell a lie is to live a lie and that is not confession or repentance.

In psalms 32:5 David says, "I acknowledge my sin to you, and my iniquity have I not hidden. I said I will confess my transgressions to the Lord, and you forgave the iniquity of my sin." Whenever David talks about his sin, it is obvious that he is greatly disturbed by what he has done and does not try to hide it. There is a difference between flaunting one's sin and being open about one's sin. Many offenders are so obsessed with the need to be the center of attention that it doesn't seem to matter how they get it, even after committing such a horrible crime, they are often unashamed and even flaunt themselves. David is greatly ashamed by his sin, but is open and honest about it.

Proverbs 28:13 says "He who covers his sins will not prosper, but whoever confesses and forsakes them will have mercy." The offender, who refuses to be open and honest about their sin has taken themselves out of the running for God's mercy. They are the ones who are turning their back on forgiveness and grace. They can demand it and plead for it, but in the end only those who truly confess and are honest about their sin will receive it. Acts 19:18 "and many who had believed came, confessing and telling their deeds." If an offender is truly repentant and open about their sin, it is possible for them to be used by God to help other offenders come to a place of repentance and confession. There is a need for offenders, who have a clear view of their sin and who are humbled before God, to reach out to other offenders and through tough love and Biblical guidelines help lead them down the same path to confession. Ezra 10:1-2 says, "now while Ezra was praying, and while he was confessing, weeping and bowing down before the house of God, a very large assembly of men, women, and children gathered to him from Israel; for the people wept very bitterly…We have trespassed against our God."

For the offender who is contemplating his life and how he is going to get right with God, it seems like this would be a good place to start. When you read this passage it is apparent to all that Israel is broken over her sin. We see no brokenness today over the sin of the offender. The offender is not broken, his friends are not broken, Christians are not broken, and the church is not broken. If there is no brokenness, there is no repentance.

Must Accept the Consequences of Their Sin

This is one of the hardest things that the offender needs to do. It goes against human nature to accept the consequences of our deeds. For the offender the consequences will come in many forms. There are legal and Biblical consequences as well as social ones. In one case that we are familiar with, the offender indicated that he was repentant and that he would do whatever he needed to do to make it right. A group of pastors who met with this person went through each of the steps that he would need to go through in order to deal with his sin and to be accountable to the law and the church as well as to the family of the girl he had molested. He agreed to submit to the leadership of the church and that he would cooperate with authorities. But the next day, instead of turning himself in, he went out and got a lawyer to protect him from the consequences of his crime. His lawyer in turn sent out letters, threatening the girl and her family with what she would go through on the stand. The offender proceeded to call various people from the church and tell them a different story, than what he had confessed to the pastors. The point is that it is easy for the offender to say that they will do whatever God wants them to do. But when it comes right down to it, most refuse to accept the consequences.

The legal penalties will be decided by a jury or a judge. But the church needs to have guidelines in place to deal with offenders. Accepting these guidelines is a must if the offender is ever to attend church again. The fact that an offender should never be around children cannot be stressed enough. No matter where the children are, the offender is always a danger, even in a public place. It may be possible for the offender to have a place where they can sit in the church, if the church is agreeable, and if there is always someone with the offender from the time they arrive at the church parking lot until the time they leave the church parking lot. The offender needs to have a mentor to be with him at all times while they are at church. If he uses the bathroom, his mentor will escort him to the bathroom and make sure no children are in there before he goes in. Far too many cases of children being molested in a public bathroom are being reported. The church must ensure the safety of the children at all times, if they cannot do that, then the offender should not attend. He may need to get his teaching and fellowship from a small group gathering, where he can worship and learn and pray with other Christians without being a danger to children. I'm convinced that if an offender will not graciously accept the boundaries that must be imposed as a result of their own criminal behavior, then they are not repentant and not sincere about getting right with God.

The children of Israel were in the process of being punished for their behavior. God had allowed most of them to be captured in battle and the few remaining Jews came to Jeremiah and wanted him to ask God, what they should do. They had told him ahead of time that no matter what God said they would obey Him. In Jeremiah 42:2-5 it says, "pray for us to the Lord your God, that the Lord your God may show us the way in which we should walk and the thing that we should do. I will pray to Lord your God according to all your words. So they said to Jeremiah, let the Lord be a true and faithful witness between us, if we do not do according to everything which the Lord your God sends us, by you."

It sounds like the remaining Jews that were left in Israel meant business when they approached Jeremiah to ask God what they should do. Just like many religious offenders who quickly give lip service to the Christians around them. He tells them what they want to hear. But when they are given the guidelines and boundaries that they will need to follow in order to maintain fellowship and contact with people from the church, they complain that their punishment is greater than they can bear. That sounds like Cain, after he killed Able and God marked him and banished him to be isolated from society. Cain said, "My punishment is greater than I can bear". When you think about Cain's crime of murder, you would think that his punishment of being banished from society would be very reasonable and yet he complained. When someone rapes a child or molests a child, the punishment should be very severe and yet offenders complain about the simplest of consequences.

When Jeremiah asks God what Israel should do, God said that they should stay in the Promised Land and that He would take care of them. You would think that would be good news for them, but the problem was they had already figured out what they wanted to do. They had already decided that the best thing for them to do was to go back to Egypt and stay there. But in the book of Jeremiah 42:10, 11 it says, "If you will still remain in this land, then I will build you and not pull you down, do not be afraid for I am with you". So when he finished telling the children of Israel what God had said, they said to Jeremiah "the Lord has not sent you to say 'do not go down to Egypt to dwell there'. So after vowing to do whatever God said they should do, they wound up doing just the opposite. They did what they wanted to do all along. Unfortunately most religious offenders are quick to say that they will do what they need to do, but most in the end, refuse to do it. So Israel left to go back to Egypt and because of their rebellion, God destroyed most of them with the sword and with disease. So too, the offender, who rebels against God's command, is destined for God's judgment.

The consequences that the judge will hand down are <u>punitive</u> in nature. In other words they will go to jail, along with other consequences that are designed to punish the offender for what they have done wrong, and that is how it should be. Punishment is meant to be a deterrent to crime and God says in Romans 13 that He expects criminals to be punished. But most of the consequences that we are talking about here are the consequences that the church and family implement and they are <u>preventive</u> in nature. In other words they are designed to prevent the offender from raping or molesting other children. Why is it, that so many Christians cannot grasp the importance of this Biblical concept of consequences?

Nathan the prophet told David that because of his sin, "the sword would never depart from his house". God even went on to say that He would raise up an adversary against David from his own house. David confesses his sin and asks for God's forgiveness. God does forgive him, but the consequences were still meted out to David by God and by those around David whom God used to hold him accountable for what he had done.

Consequences are a part of God's plan for dealing with sin. When the church and the family refuse to hold the offender accountable, they are standing against God and the victims of the offenders. If the offender is repentant, he will seek out and accept the consequences placed on him from the law, church and family, not try to avoid it. Jesus said in Matthew 12: 33-36 "either make the tree good and it's fruit good, or else make the tree bad and its fruit bad, for a tree is known by its fruit. Brood of vipers! How can you being evil speak good things? For out of the abundance of the heart, the mouth speaks. But I say to you that for every idle word men speak, they will give account of, in the Day of Judgment." If we will give account of every idle word, what do we think will happen to those who profess to be believers, and yet rape and molest children? The offender wants us to believe that they are good and yet they produce evil fruit. They want us to believe that they are a Christian and that they are right with God and yet they produce evil fruit. Jesus said the tree is known by its fruit. If the fruit is evil then the person is evil and their heart is evil. Jesus calls them a "brood of vipers" and then says to them, "how can you being evil, speak good things?" In other words the person, who is evil and yet pretends that they are good, is like a viper. They cannot be trusted. They are dangerous. They are a wolf in sheep's clothing.

If the offender is sincere about wanting to get right with God, he needs to embrace the consequences of what he has done and be determined to take full responsibility for it. Perhaps then he will find mercy before a Holy God, who has promised to hold us accountable for what we have done.

Must Labor to Make Restitution

Restitution is a lost concept today, but it was taught in God's word as a principle to live by. In Exodus 22: 1-15, God talks about this precept. "If a man steals an ox or sheep, and slaughters it or sells it, they shall restore five oxen for an ox or four sheep for a sheep". Restitution and punishment are two different things. When I was six or seven years old, I remember coming down to the breakfast table and seeing that mom had the table set and there was a half of banana by each plate. I was the first one there and was upset by the fact that we only had a half of banana. When mom went to call the others, I ate my half and took my sisters half as well. When I was caught, I received a proper punishment at the time, and then later that day, when mom gave out our evening snack, she set mine aside so that I could see it and then gave it to my sister, whose banana I had taken earlier. I remember being upset and saying it was unfair because I had received a spanking already and I thought that was punishment enough. But what I failed to realize was that the spanking was the <u>punishment</u> to teach me not to steal or take something that is not mine, but giving my sister my snack was the <u>restitution</u>, fortunately for me, mom forgot about the four or five fold that God mentioned in Exodus chapter 22.

Most victims and their families would want nothing from their offender and would certainly not want the offender to think that the restitution somehow makes up for what they did. Nothing can make up or repair the damage the offender has done, even obedience to the commandment that God first mentioned in Exodus 22. I think a good way to implement restitution, in cases of abuse, would be something similar to what 'mothers against drunk drivers' are doing by having those who have injured or harmed others because of their actions, be shown on TV while confessing their crimes and urging others not to go down the same path. There are many not-for-profit ministries, like ours (Speaking Truth in Love Ministries), who are trying to stop this evil, and funding is always hard to come by. Offenders could be mandated to take the money that they would spend on themselves and donate it to help stop abuse. This is something that would have to be a great sacrifice on the offender's part or it would be of little use as restitution. Restitution in no way eases the guilt or the punishment of the offender, but should be a requirement along with repentance, confession and accepting the consequences, before the church even considers the step of restoration. In the book of Luke 19:8 Jesus goes to a man, by the name of Zacchaeus, and says I want to go to your house today" as Jesus sits at his table, he is so convicted about his sin that he says "if I have taken anything from anyone by false accusation, I will restore it four fold". Zacchaeus knew in his heart what he needed to do and makes the commitment not only to return anything that he had stolen, but that he would restore it four fold. For the offenders and enablers who feel these restitutions are somehow unfair, perhaps they should think about the children who have been raped and molested, who will live with the shame and nightmare of what happened to them for the rest of their lives. There will be no break for them; their innocence was stolen by a selfish, uncaring person, who can never give it back. Restitution is a concept that God teaches in His word and it should be practiced today. Money can be contributed to a fund that would pay for medical help, counseling or other needs that the victims may require. Only until the offender fully follows the steps of; confession; repentance; restitution, and maintains these for the rest of their life, will they ever truly find restoration.

Must Realize that Restoration does not mean that Everything goes back to the Way it was

From time to time we get a virus on our computer and Faith will have to reset the computer back to the previous week and usually that will take care of the problem. For Faith's dad and most other offenders, they seem to think that after enough time goes by and they have said that they are sorry, a time or two, that the clock should be reset and they can now sing in the choir, interact with children, teach Bible study and go back to the way things were. When that is the attitude of an offender it shows us that their heart is still evil and that they just don't get it.

I realized as I looked back over the years, that that is exactly what most of the family and the church folks had always done. Some people would be angry and upset for a time and then after a few months or year or two, all the concern would die down and every one would let down their guard again. Without any repentance, confession, or restitution, they would simply 'reset' the offender back to his previous 'settings' before his sin had been revealed, and the people at church and in the family would act as if nothing had ever happened. Just like 'resetting' the computer, their memory is erased and they can go back to the way things were… and the offender can continue abusing children. Nothing had changed, it was like everyone would just put their blindfolds back on and pretend nothing happened.

Remember that God had Paul tell the Corinthian believers to turn the offender that was in their midst over to Satan for the destruction of the flesh that the spirit might be saved in the Day of Judgment. Offenders rape and molest over and over again because they are evil in their heart. In the book of Matthew 12:35 it says, "A good man, out of the good treasure of his heart brings forth good things, and an evil man out of the evil treasure of his heart brings forth evil things." Jesus clearly says in these verses that when someone does something evil it is because their heart is evil. Too many Christians are naïve; they think offenders are really nice people who have just made a few mistakes. There is no excuse for this kind of logic; people do evil things because their hearts are evil. And the reason they can do those evil things time and time again and get away with it, is because we refuse to Biblically hold them accountable for their deeds.

Can there ever be restoration? Yes, but that does not mean that everything will be like it was before, there must always be safeguards to protect the children. So what does restoration mean? It means that Christians can now eat and fellowship with this person because they have demonstrated that they have repented and they have made a full and godly confession, and they are accepting all of the consequences and are doing everything they can to make restitution. It means they may be able to attend church with a mentor and they can attend small groups for adults. They cannot and should not have contact with children. The guidelines and boundaries will vary from church to church, but each church needs to determine what is appropriate and Biblical. I know this seems like a gloomy outlook for the repentant offender, and does not offer the kind of hope and they are looking for. But the <u>greatest hope</u> of all for every believer as well as the believer, who is an offender, is that one day we will be rid of this old body and will be made whole and will never sin again. And we will dwell in heaven and on the new earth for all eternity. There will be no sin there, no sinful thought, and we will all be perfect without fault or flaw.

Even the Apostle Paul cried out and said "Oh wretched man that I am who shall deliver me from the body of this death? I thank God through Jesus Christ our Lord." Romans 7:24, 25. Oh yes, there can be forgiveness and transformation in this life, and that will be the hardest thing the offender has ever done. It will only come when they have diligently obeyed God's word in all of the steps that must be taken. An attempt to take a shortcut is an indication that they lack the conviction and determination to do it right. All shortcuts will lead to failure and more abuse.

Jesus said that the way to heaven was narrow and difficult and few people would find it. I think that while restoration is the goal for all believing offenders, that only a few will ever truly find it.

I cringe when I hear of victims of sexual abuse being reconciled to their offender, because the reality is that while they may have convinced their family, church and victim of their repentance and sincerity, they are most likely still molesting other children. I know this sounds horrendous to say, but here is the problem. In many of the cases that we are familiar with, where the victim says that they now have a 'wonderful' relationship with their offender, it simply means that they are getting along well and they don't talk about the past. In most of these cases there was no dealing the sin, there was no jail time, there was no repentance, no seeking forgiveness. In other words there was no real change, everything just went back to the 'way it was'. It's about power, control and manipulation, it is their game and when we are gullible enough to play it, they always win. Pray for the repentance, but always beware of their real motives.

11
The Truth

There is much debate today about truth, and whether it is relative or absolute. When people do not have a basis for truth then 'truth' to them is 'relative' or changeable. But for the Christian who understands the Bible to be the Word of God, we see 'truth' as 'absolute'. The world's perception of the truth is vastly different from the Christian's perception. Jesus said in John 17:17 "Sanctify them by your truth, your word is truth." Our understanding of truth begins with the Word of God and it will be from that perspective that I am going to approach this last chapter. I want to consider, in this chapter, the truth about Forgiveness, Mercy, Grace, Love, Sin and The Consequences of Sin. It is not what I believe about these things that is important, it is what the Bible teaches about these things that is important.

The Truth About Forgiveness

For some reason, when it comes to sexual abuse and domestic violence, Christians often misunderstand the biblical teaching on forgiveness. This creates a perfect environment for offenders to sneak in and prey on children and get away with it time and time again. We must remember that God hates sin and he does not excuse it or look the other way. If that is the case, then why is this sin so rampant in the church? God's Word is very clear that if a believer sins, God will chasten him. In Hebrews 12:8 we read: "but if you are without chastening, of which all have become partakers, then are you 'bastards' and not sons." The word *bastard* means, that someone is an illegitimate child. So what God is saying is that if someone, who claims to be a Christian, sins and God does not chasten him, then he is not really a Christian at all.

In the book of Jude verses 4 – 8 we read, "For certain men have crept in unnoticed, who long ago were marked out for this condemnation, ungodly men, who turn the grace of our God into a license to sin and deny the only Lord God and our Lord Jesus Christ." We will deal with this verse more when we get to the 'truth about grace' section, but the first part that is speaking about men who have crept in unnoticed, is what I want to deal with here. Why have they crept in unnoticed? We want people to come to church and we go to great lengths to bring them in. So why does Jude refer to these men as sneaking in and going unnoticed? It has to do with 'why' they were coming, in the first place. They were planning to commit immorality and they knew Christians would be an easy target, because of our teachings on forgiveness and grace. Our weak views on what God's Word teaches about forgiveness and grace have become a revolving door for sexual offenders to rape and molest children and we feel powerless to do anything about it because, after all, we must forgive.

In this section, I want to look at the truth about forgiveness and what it means and what it does not mean. In the book *"Surviving the Secret"* (p. 129) it says, "Absolute, pure forgiveness can be granted only when repentance is extended." For repentance to be sincere, it must be willing to look into the past. Too often I hear the phrase, "You need to forgive and forget" or what about, "You need to forget and move on." And while there is a grain of truth in both of these assertions, the reality is that we do in fact remember the sin. So have we really forgiven, if we can still remember the wrongs done to us? The question begs to be asked, whether true forgiveness must involve forgetting or remembering?"

When Faith told me, while we were dating, that her father had raped her, my first reaction was to sever ourselves from him, but after discussing the issue of forgiveness we thought that there was nothing we could do except overlook what he had done and try to keep our future children away from him. After all, that is what forgiveness is,. . . right? That is what the vast majority of Christians believe or at least that must be our conclusion, since the church in America has not been holding sexual offenders accountable for the crimes they commit against children. In reality, what we did was not 'forgiveness' at all, it was simply doing nothing. In order for there to be forgiveness, there must be an intentional effort to deal with the sin, and that was never done in our case. So let's take a closer look at forgiveness.

There are a couple of Greek words that are translated "forgive or forgiveness" in the New Testament. The general meaning of the word is to 'release or send forth.' The idea is that if someone sins against someone else and they repent and seek forgiveness, then we are to release them from any obligation to us.

The Basis for Forgiveness

First of all let's consider the basis for forgiveness. The basis for all forgiveness is what Jesus Christ did for everyone on the cross. If it were not for His sacrifice, no one could be forgiven for any wrong done. In the book of I John, we read in 1:9: "if we confess our sin, He is faithful and just to forgive us our sins." Have you ever wondered why God uses the word "just" in this verse? How can a Holy God be 'just' in forgiving our sin? It is because, when Jesus died on the cross, God the Father laid the sin of the whole world on His own son as He was hanging on the cross. In 2 Corinthians 5:21 we read: "for He made Him, who knew no sin, to be sin for us, that we might become the righteousness of God in Him." Christ's sacrifice was sufficient to pay for any and all sin. All of us are sinners and we all need God's forgiveness. Romans 3:23 says "for all have sinned and come short of the Glory of God"

Receiving Forgiveness

Even though Christ died for the sins of the world, forgiveness was not extended automatically, or else everyone would be saved and there would be no need to accept Christ. Forgiveness only counts for each individual, when they ask God for it. Christians receive forgiveness and salvation when they put their faith and trust in Christ. Even as Christians, people often still sin and they need to seek God's forgiveness. The point is that in order to be forgiven, each individual must seek that forgiveness from God. In the first book of Corinthians, in chapter 11, Paul said that because the believers at the church in Corinth were partaking of communion in an unworthy manner, with un-confessed sin in their hearts, that many of them were sick and even dead. The 'unworthy manner' that Paul was talking about with the Corinthians was not just any sin, it was specific—the well-to-do were eating their food and when the others, probably slaves or the poor came to the 'love feast', like a poorly planned potluck, they were left without any food! How would we feel? And where was the 'fellowship'? The point is that these well-off Christians were oblivious to the needy that were in their midst.

This was scandalous and hypocritical. Their sin was humiliating the poor at their love feasts and in so doing they were disrespecting the Lord's Table. If it was to be a love feast, fellowshipping around the table as believers in Christ, they needed to get with the plan and make room for these other brothers and sisters or they were totally missing the point of the fellowship meal around remembering Christ's death and resurrection. My point in mentioning this passage has nothing to do with the sin itself, but rather the fact that God would chastise an unrepentant believer even to the point of death.

The stubborn believer, who refuses to confess and repent, will be chastened by God and if they continue to harden their hearts, it may even result in death. The sexual offender is no exception, unless they make a true confession and repent, their sin remains un-forgiven. For some reason when it comes to sexual abuse and domestic violence, Christians seem to be focused on telling the victims that they need to forgive the offender. While that is true, the primary focus should be on the need for the offender to confess and repent and then to seek forgiveness.

The victim can have a forgiving attitude, but unless the offender has confessed and repented, they still remain in their condition of un-confessed (and for some, their 'still practicing') sin. Remember I John 1:9 says that, "_if_ we [believers in Christ] confess", only when there is true confession can there ever be true forgiveness. Also, we read in Luke 17: 3 that "_if_ he repents, forgive him." It is so important for the church to make sure the offender understands that forgiveness for the sins they have committed, is not automatic, it must be sought and, according to the scriptures, it must be preceded by confession and repentance.

Giving Forgiveness

Giving forgiveness is not an option; we are commanded to forgive in many places in God's Word. Forgiveness is one of the spiritual disciplines of the believer in Christ and in the church. In the Lord's Prayer Jesus says, "Forgive us our trespasses as we forgive those who trespass against us." In Matthew 18:21-35 it says, "Then Peter came to him and said, 'Lord how often shall my brother sin against me, and I forgive him? Up to seven times?' Jesus said to him, "I do not say to you, up to seven times, but up to seventy times seven. "Therefore the kingdom of heaven is like a certain king who wanted to settle accounts with his servants. And when he began to settle accounts, one was brought to him who are owed him 10,000 talents. But as he was not able to pay, his master commanded that he be sold, with his wife and children and all they had, and payment be made. The servant therefore fell down before him, saying, 'master have patience with me, and I will pay you all.' Then the master of that servant was moved with compassion, released him, and forgave him the debt. But that servant went out and found one of his fellow servants who owed him 100 denarii; and laid his hands on him and took him by the throat, saying, 'pay me what you owe!.' So his fellow servant fell down at his feet and begged him, saying, 'Have patience with me, and I will pay you all.' And he would not, but went and threw him into prison till he should pay the debt. So when his fellow servants saw what had been done, they were very grieved, and came and told their master all that had been done. But his master, after he called him, said to him 'you wicked servant! I forgave you all that debt because you begged me. Should you not also have had compassion on your fellow servant, just as I had pity on you?' And his master was angry, and delivered him to the torturers until he should pay all that was due to him. So my heavenly Father also will do to you if each of you, from his heart, does not forgive his brother his trespasses. God's Word is very clear; we must forgive those who trespass against us. Forgiveness is not an option, it is not easy, but if God forgives us, then He expects us to forgive others. What a powerful message on forgiveness. There are several things that we need to consider in this passage. First of all in this story the servant, who owed 10,000 talents, represents the sinner, or, all of us, who owe such a debt because of sin, that we could never repay it. Not with good works, or being baptized, or going to church, or any amount of effort on our part. That is why Christ had to die on the cross for the sins of the whole world.

Every sinner, who accepts Christ as their savior is like the first servant. But when he had been forgiven all of his debt, he went out and found someone who owed him a small amount of money and refused to forgive, that is, to cancel the debt. This individual in the story chose rather to sell his neighbor into slavery for not having funds to cover the debt. Just as the master was angry with the first servant, it is a picture that shows the reader that since God forgives people their great debt of sin, that He expects people to forgive all those who sin against them. In comparison, the debt of those who sin against us is much smaller than the debt all of us owe to God. For the child who has been raped or molested or beaten this may seem unfair or unkind, but God is not making light of the evil committed against us. We need to try and see our own sinful condition and our own helplessness, to do anything about it and couple that with the fact that Christ didn't have to come and suffer and die on the cross, but He did, all because He loves us.

I also want you to notice in this passage that Jesus brings out the fact that both servants "beg" for forgiveness, they both understood their plight. Unlike these characters in this story, we have noticed that many sexual offenders have a cavalier attitude and barely make an apology. One offender said "I said I was sorry, what more can I do." It is hard to believe that the arrogance and ignorance of someone who has raped or molested many children, saying "what more can I do." How about get on your face before God and beg, how about telling the truth about your sins and your crimes, how about at least having enough shame to hide your face and beg for forgiveness. If you only knew the anger of God against you for what you have done, your knees would be too weak to stand. Jesus ends this passage with the admonition that all must forgive, from our heart, those who have sinned against us. The best way to do this is to remember what God, through Christ, has done for us.

What Forgiveness is Not

The area I find to be the most difficult, when it comes to Faith's dad and those who excuse his behavior, is the line between forgiveness and holding them accountable. I want to spend some time exploring both of these issues, because I have wrestled with these questions over the past few years. Forgiveness is not saying what they have done is all right, it is not exempting them from the consequences, it is not protecting them from prosecution or punishment, and it is not saying things will go back to normal.

Faith and I made a decision a long time ago to forgive him for what he had done to her, but what we failed to do was to hold him accountable. When God tells the Corinthian believers through the apostle Paul, to "deliver such a one to Satan for the destruction of the flesh." (I Corinthians 5:2) The question that arises is: is that unforgiving? If it is unforgiving, to deliver this person over to Satan for the destruction of the flesh, then is God violating His own word? Holding a sexual offender accountable for their crime is not being unforgiving. Delivering this offender in the Corinthian church over to Satan for the destruction of his body was not being unforgiving. In the book *"Children and Sexual Abuse"* (p. 21) it says "victims must realize they can forgive without surrendering their desire for justice, 'vengeance is mine, I will repay,' says the Lord, Romans 12: 19. There will be a court date for all of those who have sexually abused children. God will be the judge, and He will meet out punishments according to the crimes." There are two entities that God has given the authority to mete out judgment, God is one and the government is the other.

In the Scriptures, there are some definite guidelines that need to be recognized. When God tells his people not to fellowship with someone who claims to be a Christian and who continues to habitually sin, is that unforgiving? When God tells us not even to eat with such a person, is that unforgiving? Then why is it that when we put God's Word into practice and hold offenders accountable for their sin and their lack of repentance that the rest of the church accuses us of being unforgiving? It is not unforgiving to obey the word of God.

In the book *"Laura"* a young girl had a father who would prostitute her for money. One of the men, who would routinely give her father money and then rape her, was a minister. Each time he would rape her, he would ask God to forgive him and she would pray in her heart that God would not forgive him. Do you think God forgave him because he made a request for forgiveness? He did not ask the girl for forgiveness, he was simply trying to ease his conscience. His request is not a confession, since confession means 'to agree with God about the sin' and he certainly was not repentant, since repentance means 'to turn and go the other way'. This despicable person continued to rape the young girl. It seems he never turned himself into the authorities or reported his crimes. If these things are true, then we must conclude, according to the scriptures, that he was not forgiven.

It says in I John 1: 9 that "*if* we confess"; only until we confess, which again, means agreeing with God about sin, does God forgive people? And then again, in Luke 17:3 it says, "If your brother sins against you, rebuke him and if he repents, forgive him." It seems as though we keep forgetting about all of the 'ifs': if we confess; if he repents. Most Christians view forgiveness as unconditional and yet in these verses the word "if" is used. Many Christians and church leaders only remember parts of these verses when it comes to teaching about forgiveness. The burden is on the one who sinned to make the confession and to show repentance. When this is done, all of us are obliged to forgive, from our hearts, the person who sinned against us-- knowing, that our forgiveness will not exempt them from facing the consequences of their actions. In most cases of sexual abuse there is no true confession or true repentance. What is a victim to do in those cases? It is very important in the healing process to have a forgiving heart and a forgiving attitude. Hate and bitterness will only deepen the pain and feeling of loss and isolation. However, forgiveness is not extended by God to the offender until he confesses and repents.

Furthermore, Forgiveness is not forgetting. A child who has been raped or molested will most likely live with that nightmare the rest of their lives. Hopefully with God's love and a renewed focus on Him, some of the memories will lessen and fade, but for church leaders to simply demand that victims of sexual abuse "forgive and forget" is neither reasonable nor biblical. Forgive yes, but forgetting is, usually, not humanly possible. There are, of course, cases where the child was too young to remember and yet still bears the scars of pain and mistrust. There are also cases where the trauma was so devastating that in order to mentally and emotionally survive, the child compartmentalizes the abuse and represses it, because the thought of it is too painful to bear. The kind of "forgetting" that I am talking about here is that when the victim comes forward for help and support, they are told they must forget. Forgiveness is a decision that each person must make in their own heart, but to say that they must forget only traumatizes the victim more, by placing a demand on them that is not humanly possible to do.

Another point that we must make here, is that forgetting is not always healthy for the victim. Victims need to deal with their abuse and they need to understand what has happened to them. When church leadership is so quick to cut off the memory and record of the abuse, they bring great harm to the one who has been abused and this interferes with the healing process. No one breaks an arm and just pretends it didn't happen or just forgets about it. They go to the emergency room and they get a doctor to put a cast on it--so they can begin the healing process. Even later in life, they can refer back to the time when they broke their arm.

Church leaders should never try and rob the victim of that need to fully deal with their sexual abuse. Yes, even to refer back to it years later-- maybe as a way to help others find their journey to healing. Those that surround the victim should be their protectors and the ones demanding justice. When victims see God's demand for justice being pursued by their protectors, it makes it easier for them to be able to forgive their offender of the personal debt that He will never be able to repay. Prison is both a punishment and a deterrent to future crime by locking the offender away from children they will not be able to commit further crimes against them.

The Truth about Mercy

Many make the mistake of thinking that mercy and justice are incompatible yet God loves both and demands both from his people. Mercy is not pretending that abuse didn't happen or ignoring it, because that would be a sin. There are a number of Greek words that are translated "mercy" in the New Testament. The general sense is that mercy means 'pity or compassion.' The sexual offenders and enablers want Christians to believe that if they are merciful that they will let them go scot-free. That would be injustice and unbiblical. God is outraged with injustice. We will get more into this when we look at the 'truth about justice'.

<u>The truth is that justice must also stand alongside of mercy or else you have neither</u>. It is not compassionate to let a sexual predator go free, in the name of mercy, only to have them rape and molest another child. It is not compassionate to the current victims who are terrified and sickened by the calls for mercy for the offender, by the same people telling them to be quiet! Who are the ones not showing mercy? The enablers brush aside the victims with no more care than running over a stray cat. They are the ones not showing mercy. The sexual offender, who wants no consequences for their deeds, is the one showing no mercy.

So then, what does mercy look like? First of all it is not taking vengeance, but leaving that up to God and the law. It is helping those who were hurt by the offenders and their crimes. It is trying to stop more sexual abuse by doing everything possible to see the offenders are behind bars, where they can't prey on children- -that is mercy. Shakespeare once said, "A rose by any other name is still a rose." Calling what is really injustice, mercy, does not change the fact that it is still injustice. Proverbs 28:13 says "he who covers his sins will not prosper, but whoever confesses and forsakes them will have mercy." In this verse God says that mercy will be extended to those who 'confess and forsake' their sin. Here we have both confession and repentance, agreeing with God about one's sin and turning away from it.

Most offenders will try and bury their sin as it is human nature, but there will be no mercy for those who stubbornly refuse to both confess and forsake abusing others. One of the offenders, that we know, started attending a new church shortly after he had molested a fourteen year old girl. He was arrested and it was in the newspapers, so he went to the new pastor to "get counseling", thinking that he would be able to talk his way out of an embarrassing situation. He explained to the pastor that it really was the girl's fault and that this was the first time anything like this had happened. The problem was that he was lying; he was hiding his sin. The pastor counseled him for a few weeks with only hearing his side of the story, but when the pastor found out that there had been many other victims, he gave the offender the opportunity to come clean with his whole life and the offender lied again, saying that this had never happened before. So when the pastor confronted him with the testimony of one of his other victims, this perpetrator was enraged that he had been found out. He was covering his sin and according to God's Word, as long as he covers his sin and does not confess and forsake it, he will not receive mercy from God.

Should we demand that the victim and the victim's family show mercy when the sexual offender is still lying and trying to cover his sin? Should they be made to feel guilty when the arrogant offender whines that they are not merciful? In the book of Jonah 2:8 it says that, "those who regard worthless idols, forsake their own mercy." This verse in Jonah indicates that the idol worshippers are the ones to blame for not receiving mercy. It is the offender who forsakes his own mercy. It is not the fault of the victims or their families. When the offender made the decision to rape or molest one of God's children, he forsook his own mercy and he should expect none. Luke 1:50 says "His mercy is on those who fear Him."

Does the person, who offends a child, fear God? The statistics show that the average offender has as many as 117 victims. How much fear of God do you think they have? Can the offender find a place of mercy before God? I think the answer is, yes, but only when the fear of God has driven them to confess all of their crimes against the victims and to forsake their evil ways. Until then, they should live in terror every day with what is awaiting them. The Bible says, "it is a fearful thing to fall into the hands of the living God." In Matthew 7:22, 23 Jesus says, "many will say to me, in that day, Lord, Lord have we not prophesied in your name and cast out demons in your name, and done many wonderful works in your name? And then I will declare to them, 'I never knew you, depart from me, you who practice lawlessness.'". No doubt there will be many religious offenders in that group of people. They will be expecting to hear God welcome them into heaven, only to hear Him say that He never knew them.

There is no mercy in hell. Luke16:24 is a story that Christ told which talks about a rich man who died and went to hell. This man, in his torment, said: "Father Abraham, have mercy on me and send Lazarus that he may dip the tip of his finger in water and cool my tongue, for I am tormented in this flame." Abraham told him that that was not possible. There is a place of mercy before God, but it must be sought in this life and it must be sought with confession and repentance or it will not be found. Remember that mercy is 'compassion and pity'; it is not the suspension of justice. If you want to show mercy to a sexual offender, pray for them and warn them of the peril they face, unless they confess all of their sins and forsake them. If you want to be merciful to a sexual offender, visit them in jail. If you want to be merciful to a sexual perpetrator, pray for them.

The Truth About Grace

We have heard some outrageous claims about the grace of God. Now to be sure, God's grace is truly amazing and without it we would all be destined for hell. Does God's grace have any boundaries? Can it really be used as a Get-out-of-jail-Free card. Or is it a license to sin? Does that seem like an unfair accusation or something no one would say or think? Then consider what it says in Jude verse 4: "for certain men have crept in unnoticed, and turned the grace of our God into a license to sin." There are people who have crept into the church and they are using God's grace as a cover to commit evil. God's grace is beautiful, but when it is used as an excuse to sin and get away with it, the sexual offender lies about and distorts the true meaning of God's grace.

In one of the churches in Pennsylvania where Faith and I had a chance to minister, the pastor had been arrested for molesting a teenage girl from the church. During one of the board meetings to discuss what he had done and how the church was going to handle it, the pastor was doing his best to minimize his actions. When one of the members expressed their disappointment in him and anger over what he had done, the pastor said that it was the "grace of God" that kept him from going any farther! So he gave God's grace the credit for only molesting the girl and not raping her. I can only imagine the anger of a Holy God, who is already outraged at the abuse of children, but then to be credited with being a part of it, is outrageous!

Then there are the times when sexual offenders think they are immune to God's anger because of His grace. I had a man in my first church that used to tell me each time he was there that I needed to preach "hell fire and brimstone." Years later I found out that he had raped all of his daughters, I was shocked, how could someone want me to preach "Hell, fire, and brimstone" when he was guilty of raping his daughters? He thought he was exempt because of the grace of God. God's grace was nothing more to him than a license to do whatever he wanted to do which was to perpetrate great harm against his own children.

It was God's grace and love for mankind that caused him to provide a means of forgiveness by sending His son to die on the cross. God wants people to repent of their sin and turn to Christ and put their faith and trust in him. To use God's grace as a reason or excuse to sin is reprehensible. In Romans 6:1, 2 it says, "Shall we continue in sin that grace may abound? Certainly not! How shall we who died to sin, live any longer in it?" In I Corinthians 15:10 the Apostle Paul commented: "but by the grace of God I am what I am, and His grace toward me was not in vain, but I labored more abundantly then they all, yet not I but the grace of God which was in me". When you look at the grace of God in Paul's life, we see that it transformed his life. Sexual offenders want to use God's grace as a type of 'force shield' to protect their evil behavior, but in truth if the grace of God was in their life at all, it would transform their life, not protect their sin. Paul says that God's grace was at work in him to make him the person he came to be. So what is the truth about grace? God's grace radically transforms our sinful condition, but it does not protect it.

Look at what God says in 2 Corinthians chapter 9:8: "God is able to make all grace abound toward you, that you, always having all sufficiency and all things, may have abundance for every good work." <u>God's grace produces good works, not evil ones</u>. The sexual offender or the enabler, who so quickly claims the grace of God, had better look again. Abusing a child is an evil work, not a good work and has nothing to do with the grace of God.

We are reminded of the stern warning found in Hebrews 10:-29 31: "of how much worse punishment, do you suppose, would he be thought worthy, who has trampled the Son of God underfoot, and counted the blood of the covenant, by which he was sanctified a common thing, and insulted the spirit of grace? For we know him, who said 'vengeance is mine, I will repay, says the Lord', and again, the Lord will judge His people. It is a fearful thing to fall into the hands of the living God". Sexual offenders, enablers, and many of our church leaders point to the grace of God whenever the issues of sexual assault and domestic violence come up--almost as though it is a magic wand that will make all of the bad stuff disappear and everyone go back to the happy times again. Grace, to them is not an attribute of the Holy God or the means by which God's plan for salvation and eternal life was given but rather it is a convenient cover for their sin.

Ephesians 2:8 reminds the reader that: "for by grace are you saved, through faith." But the unruly have come to use God's grace as a convenient wrapping or covering for their many sins. These have come to use it as a short cut that bypasses true confession and repentance, the kind where one agonizes over their sin. I can't help but think of my father-in- law and his arrogance and cockiness, claiming the grace of God and the blood of Christ. He graduated from Bible College in 1961, his daughter, now my wife was born in 1960. He started preaching in his first church while he was in Bible School. He led Faith to the Lord in 1965, when she was five years old and he started raping and molesting her when she was 9 or 10 until she was almost 18 years old. While he was pastoring different churches in the area, he was serving and taking communion with no regard for his sin. He never once asked Faith to forgive him during that whole time. When he was around 72 years of age, he pleaded guilty to molesting one of his son's adopted daughters and at that time we became aware of other reports of victims that he had raped and molested. The whole time trampling underfoot the Son of God and insulting the spirit of grace. As of the last conversation I had with him, when we cut off our relationship with him, he was completely unashamed of himself or what he had done.

The words in Hebrews 10:29-31 are absolutely terrifying. For sexual offenders who claim to be Christians and yet so disregard God's Word and force their control and lust on precious children and young people, they should be made aware of this passage and fear God. They should continually be on their face before God and their victims begging for forgiveness. How can the pastor, who spent most of his life raping and molesting children, possibly think that God's grace and favor is toward him?

After taking communion for all those years without dealing with his sin and then pretend that everything is all right, because God's grace is somehow going to protect him, is delusional indeed.

From what we read in this Hebrew's passage, it is the Spirit of God's grace that these devious wrongdoers are insulting. Only God knows for sure how many victims dad has destroyed, during his lifetime, but no matter how he twists, manipulates, and distorts the grace of God it will never cover his sin. God is not interested in covering or hiding sin, he wants to forgive it and that only happens when individuals confess, repent, and put their faith and trust in what Jesus Christ did on the cross. What does true repentance look like? Webster describes the word "penitence" as follows, 'sorrow for sins', 'implies a painful sting of conscience especially for planned sin'… Repentance adds a suggestion of awareness of one's general moral shortcomings and a resolve to change." <u>With most offenders there is no real resolve to change</u> it is only about surviving another day so that they can rape again.

Yes God wants to extend His grace to all. As a matter of fact the author of Hebrews encourages the reader to come boldly to God. See verse 4:16: "let us therefore come boldly to the throne of grace that we may obtain mercy and fine grace to help in time of need." The sexual offender as well as anyone else should seek God's forgiveness and grace, making sure that when they come that there is true confession and repentance.

So how do I show grace for my father-in- law, when he raped and molested my wife for much of her childhood? Because we have chosen to obey God's Word and are now holding him accountable for his sin, we have no contact with him, But I truly do not want to see him spend eternity in hell. I am convinced that if we only had a glimpse of hell, like the Scriptures portray that we would not wish it on our worst enemy.

I know that dad thinks that he is saved and yet when I look at the evidence in his life, I see nothing that points to God's presence. Whether or not dad is saved is in the hands of God, but I pray that someday, before it is eternally too late, that he will know what it is, to truly be repentant. My hope is that one day we will walk together in heaven, with all of our sins behind us, and our old bodies gone, with not so much as a thought of sin. All those in heaven will be redeemed and transformed children of God. That is what grace looks like to me.

The Truth About Love

Victims often hear that they are not being loving when they report the sexual offender to the law or even if they go to their church leaders to try and find help. When one victim came forward with her story of sexual abuse, in order to protect her niece from the threats of their mutual offender and his attorney, some of the seniors in her church berated her for being unloving. Nothing was said by them about the sexual offender being unloving! Church folks often have no regard for the victim or their pain.

The question remains: so who is really being unloving? Romans 12:9 states: "Let love be without hypocrisy, abhor what is evil, cling to what is good." True love, God's love, will never embrace evil. When the offender harms his victim, he is being evil, not loving. When the enablers attack the victims, they, too, are being evil, not loving. Does that seem like a harsh statement? Do you remember when Jesus told Peter in Matthew chapter 16:23 "Get behind me Satan! You are an offense to me, for you are not mindful of the things of God, but the things of men." Peter had begun to rebuke Jesus, when He was talking about His coming death on the cross. Peter was convinced that nothing like that would ever happen to Jesus. When the enablers rebuke the victims and ridicule them and call them unloving and unforgiving, they are doing the work of Satan by continuing to harm the innocent victim and justifying the evil offender. Be sure of this, that they will pay a heavy price for their deeds. They are the ones being unloving and they would do well to remember Jesus' warning in Matthew chapter 18:10: "take heed to yourselves that you do not despise one of these little ones, for I say to you that in heaven, their angels always see the face of My Father."

It is not unloving for the victim to tell their story. It is necessary for their own healing and it is not unloving for them to hope for and expect justice. It is not unloving to expect the church to obey the Word of God and to confront the sexual offender and to hold them accountable. It is not unloving to expect their church to shun the sexual offender and to set strict boundaries around them, to protect other children.

What truly is unloving is when those people, who surround the offender, try to conceal his sin while they try to relocate him to another church or town and allow him to rape and molest again. I tell you, the blood and tears of those children will be on their hands and God will deal with them accordingly. For those who doubt that, maybe you think God is a liar or just chooses to ignore His warnings, like the one and Matthew 18:10. The implication in this verse is that anyone who was thinking about harming a child had better think twice, because that child has an angel standing in the presence of God on their behalf, and anyone who even despises one of these little ones, will pay a price.

Paul's words in Romans are clear: "love does no harm to a neighbor; therefore love is the fulfillment of the law." The offenders and their enablers have done and are still doing irreparable harm to their victims. I had a meeting not too long ago, with a group of pastors who were sharing some of the difficult situations they were facing in the ministry. Each one told horrific stories of young people hooked on drugs and alcohol, immorality, and forms of self-mutilation. It was astounding to realize that in each of these cases that there had been abuse by someone from their family or church. Ephesians 4:15 is the theme verse for our ministry. It says: "but speaking the truth in love may grow up in all things, into Him who is head, Christ." When the sexual offender lies about what he has done, that is not love. When the enabler spreads the lies of the offender; that is not love. When the victim has the courage to stand up and to tell their story, in order to protect another child; that is love. When anyone finds the courage to tell the truth about this evil and confronts an offender or an enabler and thereby protect other children, that is love.

Are we so blind as Christians that we cannot understand the most basic truths of scripture? Why would any Christian tell someone who was trying to stop sexual abuse that they are not being loving? Maybe because they are only looking at the offender, and like so many, are overlooking the children who are raped and molested by them. So who has been loving and who has been unloving? We are reminded in 1I Corinthians 13:5 that: "love does not seek its own." When someone becomes a sexual offender and begins raping and molesting, what they are doing is "seeking their own." They are selfish and their selfishness turns into depravity and they become incapable of true love. To lead a selfish life is to live a life without love.

What about the enabler? Why does the enabler protect the sexual offender and reject the victim? They, too, are selfish. They are worried about themselves, they don't want to be embarrassed, and they are concerned about how this situation will impact them or their ministry. If love and selfishness cannot coexist, then the enabler is also incapable of love as long as they are being enablers. In 1I Corinthians 13:6 we read: "Love does not rejoice in iniquity but rejoices in the truth." It is one or the other. As long as our church leaders refuse to embrace the truth about this issue and what God's Word says what we must do about it, they, too, are being unloving. In contrast, for the courageous souls who God is raising up to confront this evil, who are enduring the ridicule and rejection in order to protect God's precious children, now that is what true love really is.

There is an interesting thought in this 2 Thessalonians passage. We read in 2 Thess. 2:10: "the coming of the lawless one is according to the working of Satan, with all power, signs and lying wonders, and with all unrighteous deception among those who perished, because they did not receive the love of the truth, that they might be saved." Now in these verses, God is talking about the end times and the deception that will be present, because people in the last days will reject the 'love of the truth.' I want you to see the relationship between the deception and the fact that they will not receive the love of the truth. The truth is that: 1 in 3 girls and 1 in 6 boys will be raped or molested by the time they are 18 years old and the truth is that there is little difference between the church community and the non-church community, in regards to this issue. When we embrace this truth and weep, mourn, and pray for God's forgiveness and for His help and power to change it….that is love. When God's people recognize these important factors regarding this serious situation in society and in the church, then I believe that God will respond to their pleas. To reject the truth, is to reject love and ultimately to live in deception. If we, as the church, fail to protect these children, than how can we be credible in anything we do?

The Truth About Sin

I have heard many Christians say things like: "One sin is as bad as another" or "Sin is sin". I cringe each time I hear someone say this and I know many of you will be skeptical of what I am going to say about this issue, but I would ask you to consider the Scriptures and what they have to say.

The religious sexual offenders love to use these selected terms as a way to lessen the degree of their sin and to try and make themselves seem like just an average Christian with a few bad habits. While it is true that all sin is bad and is a violation of God's law, there clearly are degrees of sin. Let's consider two primary points; the <u>punishment of sin</u> and the <u>progression of sin</u>. If we go back to the Old Testament, when God gave His law to the children of Israel, you notice that God gives different punishments for different sins. He has one punishment for stealing and another for murder and so on. In Leviticus 6:2-5 it says: "if a person sins and commits a trespass against the Lord by lying to his neighbor about what was delivered to him for safekeeping, or about a pledge, or about a robbery, or if he has extorted from its neighbor, or if he has found what was lost and lies concerning it, and swears falsely in any one of these things that a man may do in which he sins, that it shall be, because he has sinned and is guilty, that he shall restore what he has stolen or the thing which he has extorted or what was delivered to him for safekeeping, or the lost thing which he found, or all that about which he had sworn falsely, he shall restore its full value, and add one fifth more to it, and give it to whomsoever it belongs, on the day of his trespass offering."

In these cases, the punishment was the restoration of the full value plus one fifth. They needed to present it to the owner on the same day as they offered a trespass offering. Now consider the punishment for kidnapping. In Exodus 21:16 it says: "he who kidnaps a man and sells him, or if he is found in his hand, he shall surely be put to death." For kidnapping the punishment was death. If the sins were simply the same, the punishment would also be the same. In both cases, the sin is a violation of God's law, but God has the punishment fit the crime.

In Numbers 25:1-2 we read: "If there is a dispute between men, and they come to court, that the judges may judge them, and they justify the righteous and condemn the wicked. That it shall be, if the wicked man deserves to be beaten, then the judge shall cause him to lie down and be beaten in his presence, according to his guilt, with a certain number of blows." All sin is wrong, but according to God's word some sin is more egregious than others, different severities of punishment for the different severities of sin. Lying or stealing is a sin but the rape of a child is a worse sin. And shame on those who cannot acknowledge that biblical truth. Luke 12:47, 48 says: "and that servant who knew his master's will, and did not prepare himself or do according to his will, shall be beaten with many stripes. But he who did not know, yet committed things deserving of stripes, shall be beaten with few. For everyone to whom much is given, from him, much will be required." Any adult knows in his heart that it is wrong to rape and molest a child and there can be no doubt as to God's anger and wrath at such an evil act on a child. Their punishment indeed will be most severe.

We must also consider what the Scriptures have to say about the progression of sin. Sin that is not confessed and dealt with will always grow worse and worse. We are reminded of the Genesis 6:5, 6 passage which states: "then the Lord saw that the wickedness of man was great on the earth, and that every intent, of the thoughts of his heart, was only evil continually. And the Lord was sorry that He had made man on the earth, and He was grieved in His heart." Have you ever stopped to think how God must feel in His heart, as He looks down at the church today, with so many children being abused by members of the church, and still other members look the other way and do nothing?. If Jesus were to return for his children today, the fact is that His bride would not be ready. She has been lax and careless, neglecting holiness and the most basic principles of decency. There needs to be a sense of urgency for the church to be cleansed of this sin.

In reading the Old Testament prophets, it was clear that God was going to be severe in judging the sin in the land. For example, we read in Ezekiel 16:51, 52 that: "Samaria did not commit half of your sins, but you have multiplied your abominations more than they, and have justified your sisters by all the abominations which you have done. Who judged your sisters, bear your own shame also, because the sins which you have committed were more abominable than their's." Is there a difference between one sin and another? According to God's Word there absolutely is. God is saying here that the sin of Israel was worse than the ungodly nations around her.

I remember well one time listening to a pastor that I knew. When he would preach, he would get this 'holier-than-thou' tone in his voice and he would shake and rant and rave about Christians who smoke or listen to Christian rock music. I found out later, that this same person raped and molested many children, with some of his crimes being done within the church building itself. Unfortunately, it was past the statute of limitations as far as the law was concerned, but with God, un-confessed sin, that was done fifty years ago, is the same as unconfessed sin done today.

In 1I Corinthians 5:1 Paul reminded the Corinthians that: "it is actually reported that there is sexual immorality among you, and such sexual immorality as is not even named among the gentiles." Corinth was an ungodly city, but even the heathen hadn't gone as far as this man in the church, who was having sex with his father's wife. Notice how God describes this man's sin as being worse than the sin of the unsaved. Sin is always progressive, it gets worse and worse, to the point where it will destroy a person or a church or even a country. Only God knows what is in store for churches in our country if we continue down this road. <u>We must tear down this wall of silence and secrecy</u> that we have erected around the church and the issue of sexual abuse and domestic violence, and deal with this evil that so plagues our churches.

The Truth About Consequences

Most of us think of consequences as negative, but consequences are a necessary part of life. Consequences teach us not to make the same mistakes twice and they show us that sin and wrongdoing comes with a price. Children learn the difference between right and wrong by experiencing the consequences of their actions. When the church refuses to hold sexual offenders accountable, we send them the message that they can commit these crimes and get away with it. There are times when all of us are sending the wrong message to offenders, as well as to the victims. When people try to insulate sexual predators from the consequences of their sin, they are telling the victims that they are not worthy of justice. There is a need for everyone to come together and be united in holding predators accountable. Proverbs 28:17 says: "a man burdened with bloodshed will flee into a pit, <u>let no one help him</u>." When I first read this verse, I was surprised, because it seemed like God was being unfair or harsh to tell people not to help. This verse has a powerful message for the church about dealing with sexual offenders. We can pray for them, share the gospel with them, but we are not to try and break their fall or ease their consequences in any way. Now in this verse, it talks about a man that has blood on his hands and that he is headed for a pit. When we intervene and protect a predator and try to get them off with an easy sentence, we are helping to prolong their reign of abuse. God is not saying that we cannot minister to them, by seeing to it that they get counseling or spiritual help, but they are to feel the full force of the consequences of what they have done.

Unfortunately, few offenders ever truly change, even those who make a full confession and are truly repentant. Everyone must always be on guard against the perpetrator's tendencies to rape or molest. They must always have strict boundaries. If there is any hope of change or reform it will be tied to the consequences of their sin. When people protect them, they harm them. They mistakenly remove a necessary warning sign of God's impending judgment. It is similar to dealing with someone with a drinking problem. Some families try to do everything they can to protect these individuals from the consequences of what they have done and are doing, but before you know it, they are behind the wheel again and endanger the public and may wind up in jail. How much did this protective behavior really help? If the sexual offenders experience the consequences of their actions, maybe they will decide to change their behavior. Psalms 107:17 reminds us that: "fools, because of their transgression, and because of their iniquities, are afflicted."

The calamity that befalls a sexual offender, such as: a lost ministry, a broken marriage, his children having nothing to do with him, Christians who follow God's Word and break off fellowship with him, are all a result of his evil behavior and he should not be protected from them.

The following passage paints a clear picture. Proverbs 22:5 states: "thorns and snares are in the way of the perverse, he who guards his soul will be far from him." Someone, who has wisdom, will keep a careful distance from the offender. We have noticed that often when an offender is exposed, there will be so called Christians who flock to them and come to their aid. These are often, reckless people with no wisdom, who think they know what is best, but their actions only help offenders find their next victim.

What will it take before Christians will heed God's warnings? When a sexual offender finds his next victim, because of the aid of those who ignored God's warning, they in effect are as guilty as the offender. Think of all the people in the Bible, who experience the consequences of their actions. In Acts 5, Ananias and Sapphira were struck dead by God for lying to the Holy Spirit. Moses, even though he was a great man of God, was not allowed to go into the promise land, because he had disobeyed God on one occasion. God forgave him, but refused to lift the consequences, when Moses had asked for a second chance to go into the promise land. Deuteronomy 3:23 gives Moses request: "then I pleaded with the Lord at that time, saying, oh Lord God, you have begun to show your servant your greatness and your mighty hand, I prayed, 'let me cross over and see the good land beyond the Jordan'. So the Lord said to me, 'enough of that'! Speak no more to Me of this matter'." If God refused to exempt Moses from the consequences of his actions, what does God think of those professing Christians, who do everything possible to keep sexual offenders from going to jail? Moses' disobedience eventually cost him, his life. In Matthew18:6-9, Jesus gave a warning to offenders, "but whoever causes one of these little ones, who believes in me, to sin, it would be better for him if a millstone were hung around his neck, and he were drowned in the depth of the sea. Woe to the world because of offenses! For offenses must come, but woe to them, by whom the offense comes! If your hand or foot causes you to sin, cut it off and cast it from you. It is better for you to enter into life lamed or maimed, rather than having two hands or two feet, to be cast into the everlasting fire." What does Jesus mean, when He says these troubling words? Someone who offends a child is in danger of going to hell and if severing a part of your body will help keep you from offending a child then you would be better off with an incomplete body than to spend eternity in hell. Maybe it is time for Christians to think long and hard about what Jesus says.

Once again, the words of my father-in-law: "I said I was sorry, what more can I do." How pathetic of an answer, someone who raped and molested for many years, someone who took and served communion for all these years, without so much as once asking his daughter for forgiveness. And the best he can come up with is, 'what more can I do'. God has told offenders what they must do, the truth is, few if any, will ever do it.

When someone interferes with the consequences of sexual offender's sin, they interfere with God's plan to deal with their sin. Consequences can be very severe, but they are mandated in the Scriptures as a way to both deal with sin and be a deterrent from sin. In 1 Timothy 5:20, Paul reminds Timothy, who is a young pastor: "those who are sinning rebuke in the presence of all, that the rest also may fear." Offenders have good reason to be afraid, when they hear what God has to say about them. <u>If you love the offender, don't protect them from the consequences of their actions, as you may be the one helping to push them through the gates of hell</u>. If you love them, try telling them the truth and what God's Word has to say--maybe they will be terrified enough to confess and repent.

The church is not innocent on this issue, it has excused, hidden, ignored, and even been a part of this evil. It is time to tear down the wall that protects this sin and drag it out into the light. We must mourn over this sin and the pain it has caused so many, including God, Himself, who sees and hears the evil that is perpetrated on children. "Their angel's always behold the face of my father". Will you help tear down this wall? We need pastors to start speaking out against this evil and give Biblical guidelines for dealing with it. Teach it, preach it, get involved, and make a difference. For now is the time!

Let's rise up as Christians and tear down this wall together; piece by piece let's break the silence and end the secrecy that surrounds sexual and physical abuse. Let us overcome the darkness of this sin with the Light of God's Word.